I0145157

THERAPEUTIC MINDFULNESS

A Healing Skill, Not A Coping Skill

Ruth Fearnow, LMHC

Micleru Publishing

Therapeutic Mindfulness

Copyright © 2023 by Ruth Fearnow

https://www.ruthfearnow.com

All rights reserved.

No portion of this book may be reproduced in any form without written permission from the publisher or author, except as permitted by U.S. copyright law.

ACKNOWLEDGMENTS

I would like to acknowledge the many people who have bravely shared their hurts, fears and vulnerabilities with me. I would like to thank the clients, friends and colleagues who allowed me to use their stories in this book to illustrate therapeutic mindfulness in action. It is through my practice that I am able to learn about and understand healing.

There have been many authors who have inspired my growth, some of which I mention in this book. After decades of study and practice, one author's work in particular came at a critical moment. Her book tied together many concepts I'd gathered through my years of meditating and working on trauma. She deepened my understanding of mindfulness. That book is Radical Acceptance by Tara Brach. Although I have never met Tara, I owe her gratitude for supplying the catalyst which led to the process of therapeutic mindfulness.

I have been blessed with several brilliant people who have generously offered their talents to this work. The first is my long-time mentor, Dr. Livia Jansen, Ph.D, who vetted my work through a clinical lens. Next would be the spiritual leader Steven McAfee who gave feedback and schoolteacher Ani McAfee who lined the pages with "red ink" using her sharp eye and meticulous yet pragmatic editing style. I also thank my colleagues who have welcomed my presentations in our consultation group – some of whom were brave enough to volunteer!

My partner in life, Michael F. Patterson, has been a wise sounding board and endless source of support. As Michael says, iron sharpens iron and that is just one reason we are together. True partners embraces the other's gifts and uniqueness. This I have found in Michael.

This book is in honor of all those courageous individuals who are doing the hard work within themselves to make the world a better place.

CONTENTS

CHAPTER ONE

INTRODUCTION

I magine the last time an event sucked you into your own personal spiral of mental hell. What if, instead of your usual reaction, you had a special skill? What if you were able to sit and focus for a short period of time, after which you would feel calm and at ease? What if you were able to think about that same situation and it no longer had any effect on you? Does that sound like a skill worth learning?

I hope the answer is self-evident because this is what I do: I teach people how to lean in when they feel negative emotions.

Yes, I said *lean in.*

I'm being direct so you can choose now whether you need to run from this book like a caveman fleeing a pack of rabid hyenas. Therapeutic mindfulness is not the next coping skill. It will not teach you to avoid or merely tolerate your problems. It is a skill used to confront those problems directly and heal from them.

Contained in this book is a step-by-step process for resolving emotional reactions as they arise. There are also practical exercises to help you develop related skills and address areas of resistance. Therapeutic Mindfulness is not easy... but it is effective. If you are willing to face hard things in your quest to feel better, then it is time to learn how to be uncomfortable in the right way so you can find relief.

I suppose this is a lofty pitch. People don't like to be uncomfortable. If you touch a hot stove, your hand jerks back automatically. This makes survival sense. Pain is a signal of danger. Your brain is wired to protect you from danger.

By default, your brain also jerks back from emotional discomfort. In this case, pulling away from your hurt does not necessarily save you. Emotional pain about things in the past is not a signal of danger. It is a signal that something inside you needs to be repaired for you to be happy and peaceful.

When you're uncomfortable, do you do any of the following?:

- Get defensive and find someone or something else to blame

- Make your life very busy

- Focus on fixing or helping others

- Dive into social media or binge watch TV

- Berate yourself because you should be over it

- Go blank, struggle to focus

- Decide to let it go and move on by ignoring your feelings

- Focus on positive thoughts to make the bad feelings go away

- Imagine you're on a beach until the bad stuff is gone

- Run through thoughts that make you the victim so you can feel wounded indignation rather than looking at more vulnerable feelings of being hurt

When we think about our bad feelings, we often cover up the resulting vulnerability with anger, blaming, self-righteousness, or we fall into guilt and shame. All these subconscious mental tactics cover up the core feelings that we don't know how to be with.

There is no such thing as a life without pain. Learning to work with pain leads to more happiness. Don't be fooled into believing that happiness is something you either have or do not have based on what was handed to you. How completely defeating it is to think that if you've had a hard life, you don't get to be happy. This is simply not true.

We might think having a perfect story will make us happy, yet I have met people whose story looks great on the outside, while they seek me because of the tortured life they have hidden on the inside.

Happiness is not restricted to the blessed few who grew up loved in a sheltered home with few problems. Happiness is not saved for the rich or those lucky in love. Rather, some of the happiest people have earned wisdom the hard way, and found happiness. Be glad for this. If happiness is not something you can create for yourself, then you're most likely doomed before you get through puberty!

We *can* go from experiencing great pain to healing and a happier life. I want everyone to know that healing is possible. Even after experiencing absolute horror, healing is possible. Healing doesn't happen in a vacuum, however. Time does not heal all wounds. It takes more.

CHAPTER TWO

PRINCIPLES OF THE EMOTIONAL MIND

F irst, let's look at how the mind works.

While knowing the mind's patterns does not make us immune to its negative effects, awareness is necessary. Knowing the mind's patterns makes it easier to spot them when they arise. Upsetting thoughts are not fact. Rather, they are automatic mind reactions that happen to all humans.

When we pause, we have options. We can blame ourselves less and choose our responses, including the response to work with the feelings internally before responding in the world.

Split Mind

Perhaps you've never noticed, but you have a split mind. How do I know? Unless my book has become very popular with aliens, then you're human. Humans have a split mind.

Your brain represents the seat of your mind. Imagine taking your brain out and holding two halves in each hand. Look to your right hand. This part of your mind is love, kindness, gentleness, laughter, joy, peace, contentment, compassion, serenity, humility, and wisdom. It is all things calm and wise. This is your *higher self*.

Look to your left hand. This part of your brain is . . . well, it's a big jerk. In fact, it is such a jerk that it's always talking to you, trying to pull you into its misery. Imagine every moment of negativity you've had: anger, envy, jealousy, insecurity, hate, greed, arrogance, despair, self-pity, judgment, resentment, guilt, and shame. Welcome to your *jerk brain*. This is the part of your mind that operates from fear.

If you are ever unsure what side of your mind is at work, just ask yourself, "Is my mind peaceful? Or is it in turmoil?"

Consider a current dilemma you are facing. This could be a decision about a job, a romantic relationship, or whether to confront a loved one about a conflict. The dilemma could be about whether to say "yes" to a request. We always have choices: focus on one about which you feel some uncertainty and try Exercise 1.

Exercise 1. Decisions

Choose a pending decision about which you are unsure.

1. Breathe deeply, visualizing that you are breathing in calmness and breathing out stress.

2. Continue until your mind feels calmer and more focused.

3. Imagine the decision you are considering.

4. Ask yourself, "If I make this decision, does it feel peaceful or does it feel like it comes from a place of fear?"

5. Rather than judge your choice, notice any fear and how it influenced your decision. Or notice how it felt to make a decision without fear.

*Note: Any fear that comes up is a good target for the therapeutic mindfulness process as described later.

A content feeling *always* accompanies decisions from the higher self.

Fear drives your jerk brain: The fears are many: fear that we aren't good enough, fear that others will see what we are and that our shame will be justified, and fear of being weak, which leads to defense and anger. All the negative feelings have roots in fear.

Your jerk brain runs on auto-pilot. Remember the Energizer Bunny? Yeah, that's jerk brain. It can run amok literally all day and all night, day after day spinning narratives that keep you depressed, anxious, resentful, or whatever personal hell it chooses at that moment. You don't need to actively feed it; it does this on its own. When you allow your jerk brain free run of your head space, you are miserable.

Fortunately, we all have access to our higher self. It's there whether or not you've spent time accessing it. Although your higher self is always there, your jerk brain is louder. Your jerk brain blows up out of anger or screams in panic or drowns in despair. Sound dramatic? Again, welcome to jerk brain! Jerk brain wants your undivided attention. It wants you to freak out, to buy into the madness. It's as if jerk brain is its own entity and will do anything to survive.

In the moments when you calm the storm and look beneath the mental chaos, you will always find a tranquil place. This might sound strange if you've never delved into meditation or contemplative prayer. When I've guided my clients through a simple visualization, those new to such practices were often astounded by how calm they were capable of feeling—and how quiet their normally anxious brain became.

It's as if your higher self says, "I'm here. I'm always here. When you're ready to be with me, I'll still be here." When you connect to your higher self, the calmness is waiting, regardless of what is happening in the world. This is one reason mindfulness and meditation have become so popular and widespread. Whether you prefer Christian meditations, meditations on chakras, or a simple visualization sitting on a tropical beach, mindfulness practices like these connect you to a powerful and peaceful part of your mind.

The following exercise is an example of a basic but often powerful mindfulness practice to help you feel grounded in the present moment.

Exercise 2a. Here-and-Now Mindfulness

Recommended time: 2–5 minutes.

1. Go to a place where you can be alone and feel safe. Take a moment to notice your surroundings. Notice what is happening here and now.

2. Notice being here. For this exercise, here means your current location. This could be within a room where you are alone or an area where you are sitting by yourself. Here does not include events or people that are not in your immediate vicinity. This means if you are worried about what someone else is doing, you are not here.

3. Notice being in the present: being here now. For this exercise, now means these two seconds. In these two seconds, is anything wrong? Is anything bad happening right now? Once the moment has passed, you're in the next two seconds. In these two seconds, is anything wrong? Each now is just two seconds long.

4. Ask yourself: right here, in this place, and right now, in these two seconds, is anything wrong at all?

5. If this question brings a sense of calmness, pause. Notice. Notice the lack of bad things to worry about that are right here and now. Notice feeling okay and even peaceful in this moment. Right here, right now, there is nowhere else to be, nothing to fix, nothing to do. You simply get to notice feeling calm.

6. Notice what it is like in your body to feel calm here and now.

7. Notice what it is like in your head when you realize things are okay.

8. Sit with the calmness for a few minutes. Memorize this feeling.

Being present is being here where you are and in the present moment. As you practice this, you might start to realize that almost every moment in our lives is a moment where nothing bad happens. If you did not find this peaceful, take note of where your mind was wandering. It may have been consumed with the past or future, or with something happening elsewhere. You can try to direct yourself back to the here and now. You can also write down what kept you from being present and use that as a target for the emotional work described later in this book.

Exercise 2b. Extended Here-and-Now Mindfulness Practice

If you would like to extend this practice, try the following:

1. Repeat a mantra to keep focused on this feeling. You might say, "Right here, right now, I am just fine." Or you could say, "I notice the peace in my mind and in my body."

2. Enjoy this moment of peace.

3. Write the mantra on a sticky note placed where you will see it regularly or as a pop-up phone reminder. To extend the sense of peace into your day, repeat the mantra several times an hour, pausing briefly to notice how it feels.

A note on mindfulness practices: if you are often unhappy, your thinking habits contribute to your unhappiness. To help change your mind, you must practice spending time with your higher self. This book focuses on the more neglected issue of how to work through negative emotions. However, it is also important to feed the positive side of your mind. There is an overview of ways to do this in chapter 14, "Positive Psychology."

If you've never tried a mindfulness exercise, hopefully you've just experienced what it's like to temporarily suspend all your worries. If you're an experienced meditator, this might be a useful "quickie" meditation when you're short on time. It's great when you're in the car or standing in line or when you get caught up worrying about someone else.

The goal here is to become aware of your jerk brain and connect to your higher self. If your jerk brain is the source of pain and suffering, noticing it is an important step. Awareness of your jerk brain's patterns will also help you see parts of you that you can heal with therapeutic mindfulness. If your higher self is the source of contentment, peace, and happiness, it makes sense to spend time connected to it.

I imagine many people who read these exercises will nod enthusiastically and will agree intellectually, but I urge you to physically put down the book and spend a few minutes trying them before you move on. The exercises in this book build upon each other. Ideas cannot replace experience. I've had many people appear convinced when I share ideas about mindfulness practices, yet those same people are surprised moments later by how the practice feels. Experience is essential. And trust me—it feels good to take a break from jerk brain.

In general, becoming a happier person has to do with both using positive practices as well as facing the difficult, negative things. Doing the exercises above, as well as exploring meditations on YouTube can help develop your positive practices. Therapeutic mindfulness will focus on the lesser known, second part of that equation: facing the difficult, negative things.

If you practice both sides of this equation and use therapeutic mindfulness to heal the tough things that come up, not only will your skill improve, but also you will be able to work through your jerk brain reactions. Things that used to cause pain will start to feel neutral. You won't react as intensely or as often. Soon you'll find yourself spending more time feeling like your true, peaceful self.

Emotional versus Logical Thinking

We humans are all capable of feeling and thinking. In Western culture, we place great emphasis on thinking. We use logic to solve problems—especially when we are intensely emotional about them. Logic is safe. With logic, we believe we can figure out why so we can find a solution and the problem will go away. Somewhere deep down, we believe if we can fix a problem with logic, we won't have to feel the pain that came with the problem. We analyze because we don't want to feel.

We analyze because we don't want to feel.

Unfortunately, this does not work. *You can only solve a problem at the same level it exists.* Emotions and logic are different levels of the mind. You can't solve an engineering problem with emotion. It requires logic and reasoning. The reverse is also true. You can't solve grief with logic. This requires courage and compassion.

Does it sound believable to you that we can't solve a deeply emotional problem with logic—or with action? Consider this story:

Mia had felt powerless for so many years that it had become engrained in her mind. As a young woman, she earned a black belt in martial arts so she could stop feeling powerless. She felt confident and believed she could use these skills were she ever assaulted. One night after work, she had a blind date planned. At the end of the night, her date became aggressive and she was raped with ease. She didn't move a muscle.

How is this possible?

Perhaps you've heard of the fight, flight or freeze response? This is what happens when an animal senses danger. The brain takes over and does what it believes is needed to survive.

Human brains are the same. When we perceive danger, our brain takes over our nervous system with a fight, flight, or freeze response. This woman froze, literally paralyzed by fear. She was mentally and physically incapable of moving. Her emotional brain perceived a threat and took control of her body, just like a rabbit holding perfectly still when spotting a predator. Mia's brain had learned that if she wanted to get out alive, she must not provoke her attacker. For years she had practiced this survival pattern. Because her emotional brain believed this so completely, it took her logical brain offline, so to speak.

In this state, her martial arts training was useless. She could not even try to fight back.

In Western society, we think logic and action can save us. We lean on reasoning to solve problems. When the problem is linked to deep emotional wounds, reasoning is limited. This is because our need to survive, and hence our fight/flight/freeze response is more powerful than logic every day of the week.

Besides, if logic were enough, we wouldn't have problems. We would just ask Aunt Bertha or Uncle Mack for advice, hear a sensible answer, follow the advice, and move on. Problem solved.

However, we know it doesn't work this way. We all know a person who makes the same mistakes over and over again—even when they know the mistakes are causing them pain. We might get frustrated when that person comes back for advice on the same issue, agrees emphatically, and then makes the same painful decision yet again! If this drives you nuts, don't take it personally. It was never about the advice. They thought they could solve the problem with the right logic. They didn't know that you cannot solve a deeply rooted emotional problem with a logical solution.

You cannot solve a deeply rooted emotional problem with a logical solution.

If this seems hard to swallow, you're not alone. When I was in school, I had an internship where the therapy interns discussed cases with a licensed clinician. One intern brought up domestic violence. Our supervisor asked us, "What do we do when a consenting adult chooses to be in a relationship with a physically abusive partner?" The interns made suggestions to get the abused partner out of the situation. One intern asked, "Can't we just tell them to leave?"

If you've been close to someone in an abusive relationship, you know that this well-intentioned idea would not work. The person has heard this same opinion from friends or family, and some have even heard it from their own lips. Many abused partners leave the relationship only to obsess over their abuser and struggle to not return. And worse, they cannot stay with a healthy partner. Why?

These patterns are as old as dating. While understanding this particular emotional pattern would take a separate discussion, it suffices to say that the problem is rooted in deep emotional beliefs that cannot be swept away with a few words. When an abused partner doesn't return, they often find themselves abused by a new partner later.

Because their beliefs are so deeply embedded, abused partners feel powerless to change their patterns. I've met a few people who stopped dating altogether for well over a decade to avoid another abusive relationship! This was the only way they could stop the cycle. Others slowly change the pattern over decades, yet when someone does deep emotional work, everything changes. A previously abused person no longer feels the need to re-enact the old pattern.

One woman told me, "It's as though the string that tied my heart to him was cut. Now when he uses the same old lines, I feel nothing. He has no effect on me."

Deep emotional reactions come in other forms as well. Some people can suddenly fly into a rage (the fight response). Others feel intense fear at the slightest hint of conflict and will avoid it at all costs (the flight response) or they become passive (the freeze response).

This brings us to one of jerk brain's favorite tricks. When our emotional brain takes over and we repeat the same bad decisions, jerk brain spirals into a blame-fest. It says things like the following:

- "That was stupid. Why couldn't I just do what I said I would?"

- "I should be over this by now. I'm so weak."

- "There I go again. I know better. I deserve what I get."

- "I can't even do this right. I'm a failure."

Welcome to the classic shame spiral. Unless we've figured out this trick, we believe it's our voice and we become angry at ourselves. We might then obsess about how to change things because we still think we can use logic to fix an emotional problem. Yet if you pit logic against powerful emotion, emotion wins every time.

If you pit logic against powerful emotion, emotion wins every time.

Have you ever tried to use logic with someone in a full panic? Say you have a friend with a needle phobia. You accompany this friend to the lab to provide emotional support, but she starts panicking. You see her knee bouncing at light speed as she waits to be called. Then she marches dutifully to the blood draw room, turns pale as the needle punctures her skin, and promptly faints.

If logic was the key, you could've simply told her that you've done your research and learned that serious injury or death from a blood draw is less than .01 percent. You could show her the data. Even if she believes you or looks it up for herself, I don't imagine your friend will hear this information, breathe a huge sigh of relief, and calmly watch the needle penetrate her arm. Logic is not helpful against deep fear.

I saw this firsthand during a brief stint as a phlebotomist as I interned at a military base. These strong young men were determined to tough it out through sheer willpower. Luckily, the lead phlebotomist was experienced enough to see when a patient was about to faint. I still remember the first time he called out, "We have a fainter!" The other phlebotomist and I looked over and saw a young man's body go slack, sliding down the chair. We caught him in time to avoid possible injury and carried him to a reclining blood draw chair nearby.

Let's check the score:

Emotion = 1, Logic = 0

This scenario is an extreme example of flight in the fight/flight/freeze response, yet I was told that fainting was common, especially with military men. If logic could overcome intense, subconscious, illogical fear, then that young man's determination would have worked. It did not work. When the mind believes it is fighting for survival, it can literally turn off the body.

Such examples are endless. Here are things I've heard over the years that show when emotion is in control:

- "I know I should let it go, but I just can't!"

- "When my work phone rings, I immediately feel stressed. It doesn't make sense. I know I'm good at what I do."

- "Every time my boss raises his voice, I freeze. I know I'm not in danger. I guess I'm just too sensitive. I can't handle loud voices."

- "When I see anyone I know walking toward me, I immediately start sweating. My anxiety skyrockets. I know they like me, and we always have good interactions. But I start rehearsing right away what to say and how to say it. After they leave, I run the conversation over and over in my mind, looking for mistakes."

- "It's hard to admit I'm afraid of my husband. I know I want to leave him, but I feel guilty. He doesn't have anyone."

- "I know that what he did was wrong, but I feel so guilty, I cave anyway."

- "I don't even want to be with her, but the moment I try to walk away, I become terrified that I'll be alone forever."

- "I want to stand up to her, but when I try, I feel so selfish. I just can't do it."

Where does emotion control your life? Consider times you had intense emotional reactions and then berated yourself because you believed you "should have known better." Have you ever found yourself doing the following:

- Going back to a bad relationship even though you know it's an emotional disaster?

- Failing to stand up to your boss or to a parent (or someone else) in small ways that seem easy for others?

- Being irrationally afraid of being alone, rejected, confronted, or disapproved of, to the point that your decisions are made by your fear?

- Becoming irrationally angry at the slightest hint of criticism?

Whether your Achilles' heel comes up as panic, anger, relationship issues, or something else, notice when and with whom your emotions run the show. These are the same places where logic will not work. If emotion trumps logic, then emotional problems need an emotional fix.

If emotion trumps logic, then emotional problems need an emotional fix.

Another way to tell when feelings are running the show is when your decisions change with the tide of emotions. For example, when someone ends a romantic relationship while emotions are high, the breakup is often temporary. Once the anger or hurt subsides, other emotions return, such as loneliness or guilt. However, when someone is calm at the time they decide to leave, there's a better chance the breakup is permanent.

Therapeutic mindfulness approaches problems at the emotional level. Using this method, you can work on an emotional problem at the level where it exists. When emotions intensify, the emotional cause needs to be healed first. Then and only then can we use that logical brain we value so very much.

The Pain Adds Up

"I should be over this by now."

If I had a dollar for every time I've heard this statement . . .

Perhaps you've heard the adage, "Time heals all wounds." That's wishful thinking if ever I've heard it. Time does nothing of the sort. I've had a client cry when sharing a trauma memory from fifty years ago. Time gives an illusion of distance, yet old wounds come up again and again. Pain will not be ignored. If we suppress emotions, they take on disguises and then resurface. Old wounds can become so unrecognizable, we need a therapist to help sort them out. If a person doesn't heal a wound, it will wait. And wait. And wait.

You carry the pain of every unhealed hurt that's happened—it all adds up. Grief is a perfect example. You can gain some distance from the grief, but if you've never opened up to feeling and therefore healing the grief, you still carry it. All of it. New deaths will open the wound of old grief, which explains why one client tried to force himself to attend a funeral and instead fainted in the bathroom at the funeral home! The one thing he could never face was a traumatic death from his youth. As an adult, he couldn't face any grief.

If you've talked to someone who has had difficulty with grief, you'll know how that grief surfaces repeatedly. Anniversaries, birthdays, places, songs or television shows, scents, and shared hobbies can all incite a resurgence of grief. Holidays bring a sense of dread. As one client told me, "I thought I would be over it by now." Each time it surfaced, she bemoaned still being plagued by her grief, then returned to being so busy in life she couldn't feel. Since she had never worked through the pain, it was still there. Pain is patient: it will wait.

Think about what this means for people who do not work on personal growth. Every life lesson, every adversity, every painful event adds up. When someone has substantial traumas in their life, they end up with an intimidating load of pain to work through. In the beginning, this work can seem daunting and overwhelming. The work begins slowly as they build the skills, such as therapeutic mindfulness. Over time, they start to learn that they can survive being in contact with pain. Eventually, they see how the pain is far easier to deal with head-on than when it accumulates like baggage in an overstuffed suitcase.

The belief that emotions are dangerous and to be avoided at all costs is detrimental to a happy life. Consider this case:

Dorothy was great at being strong for others. Her work at an elder care facility meant helping families through hard times. When it came to her own life, however, she didn't do emotion. By her thirties, she had lost two close family members and was deeply bereaved. Because of her extreme avoidance, her buried grief had festered. More than a decade later, she arrived in my office struggling to stop an obsessive thought pattern.

As we explored her obsession, we discovered that her obsessive thoughts came from the unaddressed grief. I explained what this meant in terms of treatment—facing her feelings. This was not pleasant news for Dorothy. She could feel that her grief was present, even after all these years. For the time being, her obsession stopped, but she did not like having grief on the surface, nor did she like the idea that she had to deal with the grief to resolve her painful thought spirals.

After a few sessions, Dorothy stopped coming in. A month later, though, she was back. The obsessive thoughts had returned. It took most of the hour to break through her thought patterns, and Dorothy realized again that the underlying emotion was connected to her grief.

This pattern repeated. Each time, Dorothy would stop therapy, then return for help with her obsessive thoughts. It's as if she remembered I was able to help pause the thoughts, but she forgot why. Each time we met, she would realize with amazement that the emotions beneath her obsession led directly to her grief. She would promise to take my suggestions and work with them on her own. On one occasion, she became tearful but insisted she would "cry at home" so I wouldn't press her to feel her sadness.

Months after this incident, she returned to my office once more with a resurgence of obsessive thoughts. She was reminded yet again that her pain was connected to suppressed grief. This was her last visit.

The pain that you haven't worked through is still with you. Therapists have a saying: "What you resist persists." I also say: "What you push down will push back."

What you push down will push back.

We can squash our emotional pain so completely that we don't recognize where it comes from. We can fool ourselves. In fact, that's the purpose of emotional defenses. If we don't recognize it, we don't have to think about the original memory that caused so much suffering. The disguise protects us from what seems unbearable. Sounds great, right?

The problem is when pain builds until it sneaks out—or explodes. This can range from tears that come "out of nowhere" to violent rages to crippling phobias. In more extreme cases, a person is besieged by complex and sometimes debilitating mental health issues that seem difficult to figure out—and that's because the purpose of those issues is to express the pain while covering the cause.

When we do this, the memory might seem emotionally neutral or completely banished from conscious thought. I've heard someone say, "Oh, I've moved past that," only to learn how heavily their past impacts the present. The irony is that we push the memory away to avoid the pain of it, yet the pain is the part that stays.

Pain is insistent: one way or another, *it will be heard.*

To demonstrate this, imagine a cloth storage cube. What would happen if you filled that cube up to the top, then took a blanket and tried to stuff it by shoving everything down with all your weight? Imagine the sides bulging, the seams ripping under the pressure . . . until the contents burst through the sides.

In this scenario, the "stuff" in the cube is your emotions. The cube is you.

When emotions burst out, they might cause the following:

- Phobias

- Addictions

- Panic attacks

- Rage attacks

- Eating disorders

- Headaches

- Nausea

- Ulcers

- Physical pain

The mind can impact the body in shocking ways. Some people have reported blurred vision or even becoming temporarily blind during panic attacks. In two extreme cases, clients were referred to me for therapy by ophthalmologists because their macular degeneration had no physical cause. I was informed that it is common to refer such patients to therapy.

Emotions will be heard. Whether consciously or subconsciously, if emotions are pushed down, ignored, or denied, they will find another way to surface, but they will not be silenced.

The bottom line is this: developing the ability to confront tough emotions is vital to mental health. Slowly working through such emotions is necessary if you want to be free of their effects. Rather than run from these feelings, you can learn to move toward them. This is a skill that you can develop and eventually master. I have found that after enough practice, clients become confident that they are stronger than their pain. After this tipping point, they are able to do this work on their own. Those who keep practicing can do much of their healing independently of therapy.

The Body Keeps the Score

This heading is an homage to a book I refer to as "The Trauma Bible." Its author, Bessel van der Kolk, has a deep grasp of the interaction of mind, body, and trauma. Your body speaks your feelings and physically holds on to any that have not been processed. It keeps score—of your hurts, your trauma, your baggage.

Your body holding old emotions is a key concept to why therapeutic mindfulness works. Because unprocessed emotions are stored in your body, we can go to the body to heal.

Perhaps you have never considered how your emotions are expressed in your body. Consider what happens when you get anxious. Some people feel much of their anxiety in their chest. As panic rises, their breathing becomes quick and shallow. Their heart races. Their chest tightens. Perhaps their hands shake or sweat. Other people feel anxiety primarily in their gut. Their stomach twists and turns or they feel nauseous and might even vomit. Some people give themselves ulcers from all their gut-clenching anxiety.

Consider these common phrases that indicate ways we feel both positive and negative emotions in our body:

- "It felt like I got punched in the gut."

- "My heart was pounding."

- "I'm such a hothead."

- "I was shaking all over."

- "I felt the weight of the world on my shoulders."

- "It was like I couldn't breathe."

- "I had butterflies in my stomach."

- "I was about to burst with excitement!"

- "It took my breath away."

- "I felt like a limp noodle."

- "I was as light as a feather."

In these words, we can identify grief, shock, fear, anxiety, anger, sadness, love, surprise, relaxation, and excitement. We feel them in our stomachs and chests, on our shoulders, and in our jaws.

You might already know what you feel physically when you are sad, angry, or scared. If you practice checking for emotions in your body (as outlined in this book or using other methods), your awareness of how emotions show up will expand. Some people are less aware of their body's reactions. The more awareness you have, the more quickly you can recognize negative emotions and work through them—giving you control over your mental life.

Consider these examples:

Sam was so disconnected from his body that I had to point out repeatedly when tears appeared on his face. Bewildered, he would reach up to feel the wetness on his cheek. I would point out that he also started yawning compulsively whenever I brought up an uncomfortable subject. It took years before he accepted the connection between his yawning, the tears, and uncomfortable emotions.

*

Joyce was a very shy musician who had avoided frightening feelings since childhood. She had learned to mentally disconnect so completely that she had blocked out a recent performance. She remembered being off stage before the event, and she remembered leaving afterward. This scared her enough to tackle the problem in therapy.

In general, Joyce's mind would push feelings away so much that when she did feel them, they were nowhere near the core of her body. For many months, she only felt in her arms and hands. As she practiced facing her emotions in therapy, this evolved. She started feeling things in her chest. At the close of therapy, she'd gone eight months without a panic attack or disconnecting her mind from her body.

Because the body expresses emotions that we don't want to feel, some people become very disconnected from their body experience, only to have strong emotional reactions when having a massage or trying yoga. As the saying goes, what the mind suppresses, the body expresses.

This concept of mind-body connection extends to the medical field: We've been told that anger or stress can increase chances for heart disease, digestive issues, ulcers, or chronic pain, just to name a few examples. Because the mind and body are connected, there is a reverse effect, such as meditation reducing physical pain. I've had many clients who developed a headache or nausea that resolved minutes later as we worked through some emotion.

One client experienced temporary blindness (for about twenty minutes) when she had a panic attack. As we worked through her trauma she thankfully no longer had episodes of blindness.

Feelings will not go away of their own accord. They are saved and expressed, one way or another. If you don't deal with them, your body will express them. You can start by gaining awareness of what you feel and *where it is in your body*.

What if you changed your entire external world? Could you avoid feelings then? I had a client who tried that:

> George struggled to live in society. Relationships were uncomfortable and always ended badly. He was so determined to get away from the emotional triggers of life that he lived "off the grid" and away from civilization for years—the ultimate solution.

> Without people, the isolation ate away at George. Eventually, he returned to society, got a job, and started dating a woman. Sure as rain, he encountered all the familiar habits, relationship dynamics, and pain he had been avoiding. It was all there, waiting for him. That's why he finally came to therapy.

When you avoid problems, they wait for you. In the meantime, all your unresolved issues will keep you from being fulfilled.

If you don't feel you are in touch with your emotions—or if you feel so in touch that you are often overwhelmed—a great starting point is to practice briefly checking in with your body, as described in Exercise 3. The long version, Exercise 3a, helps you explore how to check in with your body. When you're ready, you can move to the short version, Exercise 3b.

Exercise 3a. Body Check-In (long)

This exercise will help you identify different sensations and develop language to describe what you're feeling.

Caution: if you find this exercise overwhelming, seek a therapist to help you go more slowly and to learn to contain your emotions when necessary. Similarly, if you feel spacy and like you're not yourself or not in your body, this might mean your mind does not feel safe. Please listen to your instincts and stop. Then seek a trauma-informed therapist to help you slowly ease toward the ability to connect with your body.

Body Check-In. Five minutes or less. Practice daily (or more) until it becomes a habit to check in with your body. Regular practice will help you enhance body awareness.

1. **Describe what you feel physically in your shoulders.** This might be positive or negative. Do your shoulders feel:

    ◦ Heavy, like a weight is pulling on them? Or light?

    ◦ Tight? Neutral? Or loose and relaxed?

    ◦ If they feel neutral, is it a blah feeling (which is subtle but negative), or a calm and peaceful feeling?

    ◦ If they feel loose, is there a sense of anticipating stress? Or is it a soft, relaxed sensation?

2. **Describe what you feel physically in your chest.** Notice:

    ◦ Does your breathing feel shallow or deep?

    ◦ Is your chest tight or open, light or heavy?

    ◦ Is the feeling uncomfortable or pleasant?

    ◦ If it feels neutral, is that a nice, calm feeling? Or is it a blah feeling?

3. **Scan other parts of your body and look for sensations.** For those to whom this exercise is strange and awkward, here is a list of possible sensations that are

commonly found in different body parts:

- **Head:** achy, heavy, tired, swimming, tight or loose in the jaw, sensation behind the eyes, pressure, spinning, airy, open, relaxed

- **Stomach:** tight, knotted, heavy, weighed down, cavernous, empty, swirling, nauseated, moving, relaxed, open, calm

- **Arms & Legs:** tense, tight, heavy, shaky, restless, nervous, prickly, relaxed, calm

4. Take a moment to notice what it is like to be in touch with your body sensations.

- Choose a time daily in your routine to practice this. You might try it just after you wake, before you sleep, when you brush your teeth, or in the car before driving home from work.

- If instead of body sensations, you see imagery such as a brick in your gut or a cloud in your head, this is not wrong. Try not to judge. Just go with the impressions that come up. Some people give me vivid descriptions of what the sensations are like. There might be a cage around the ribs, holding very tight, or waves in the stomach, moving fast or slow.

Your body speaks its own language. There is no need to censor or judge what comes up. Your job is simply to observe.

Once you are comfortable with the long version of this exercise, it should become easy to check in quickly wherever and whenever you find helpful.

Exercise 3b. Body Check-In (short)

1. Ask yourself what you feel (positive or negative).

2. Ask yourself where you feel that in your body.

3. Sit with it for a few moments, just noticing what it is like but not trying to change anything.

4. Continue with your day.

This exercise can help you get acquainted with the feelings in your body. Naming or describing the sensations has a power that we'll use during therapeutic mindfulness. Once you can check in and quickly find the emotions in your body, you can start using the short version – Exercise 3b – wherever you are. It can be a powerful way to gain stability, as the young lady below discovered:

> Sarah was a woman in her early twenties whose childhood pain led to drug addiction in her teens. For years, she had been attempting to heal with meditation but continued to struggle with a deep sense of emotional instability. One core belief she held was, "I can't handle this."
>
> One day she called me for an emergency session just a day before her regular session. The feeling of instability had been triggered and she was frightened.
>
> I'd recently heard a neuropsychologist say we can create calming neuropathways in the brain by practicing a brain-calming activity, such as yawning, every twenty minutes. I suggested that Sarah do a quick check-in with her body every twenty minutes if possible. She found this easy because she was a self-described "clock watcher" due to her distaste for her job.
>
> The next day, she asked herself every twenty minutes what she felt and where she felt it in her body. She could do this exercise without interrupting her daily tasks. At our session that evening, she reported feeling a

sense of stability that surprised her. By the next week, she felt more stable than she ever had before.

This became a turning point in how she saw herself. Instead of, "I can't handle this," she started to believe she was capable. She continued doing this over the next week, then reduced her practice to every thirty minutes, then to every hour only at work. She continues to use these check-ins (described in Exercise 3b) as part of her overall wellness.

If you're already stable and comfortable in your body, that's great! You can use this exercise as needed to notice when you have a strong reaction and save that issue for therapeutic mindfulness. If you do not feel stable, make this a daily practice until it becomes a habit.

CHAPTER THREE

THE THREE STRATEGIES OF THE EMOTIONAL MIND

(S)He who can sit with waves of discomfort ceases to be ruled by negative emotions.

A s discussed in the last chapter, we cannot use logic to fix deep emotional distress. You might find this hard to swallow. I get it. After all, logic is so . . . so very logical. Logic is comfortable. It tells us we can analyze our way through struggles. It convinces us that we can find the answer. It comforts us with the conviction that we can control all contingencies. With logic, we feel calm, cool, and collected. We've got our stuff together.

All lies.

Your mind does have default strategies on how to deal with difficult emotions. Unfortunately, they fall short. There is a better way, but most humans simply don't know about it. Therefore, most humans can't teach it to their children, so they grow up with protective layers around their vulnerable parts.

Our mind tries its best to help us deal with difficult emotions that it feels may be harmful to us. It wants to help, but its default strategies are not healthy long-term. We might survive, but we won't thrive.

Below are the strategies we can use to respond to painful feelings. By understanding how our mind works, we can recognize our patterns and make new choices.

Strategy 1 – Swallow

When you touch a hot stove, what happens? Your hand jerks back. You don't think about it; it happens automatically. It's a protective mechanism.

The mind reacts the same way to strong emotions. When it touches something too intense, it jerks back. Then it tries to hide the pain from us. This is the first coping strategy of our mind: to swallow bad feelings. Unfortunately, if we always retreat from emotional pain, we practice being afraid of it. The more we react with fear by running, the more our mind strengthens this avoidance.

Avoidance is no small issue. We already know that swallowed feelings add up over time. The fear of facing them also adds up. On top of that, the *judgment about having the feeling* (i.e., I'm weak/stupid/defective) is added to this pain cocktail.

On a physical level, avoiding pain and pursuing pleasure have their uses. Consider a caveman's physical preservation: the pain of walking on thorns is bad (it could lead to infection and death), and the pleasure of eating apples is good (it keeps you alive).

On an emotional level, this principle leads us astray. Avoiding scary things gives short-term relief but reinforces fear. Over time, we find more and more things to avoid until we are paralyzed in everyday situations.

Our mind's deeply ingrained penchant for avoidance is the same with all negative feelings: you might be comfortable with sadness but avoid anger or vice versa. Even so, when emotions intensify, the mind tries to protect us from feeling.

If we want to identify and heal our hurts, we must develop a keen awareness of our avoidance patterns, because the mind has ingenious ways to avoid pain.

When I was in elementary school, I used to get "bellyaches," and I would get to stay home. I still remember my last bellyache. I had just started middle school. One day I felt unwell and asked my mother if I could stay home. She asked her standard question, "What are your symptoms?" When I told her my tummy hurt, that wasn't enough to convince her I was sick. She told me I had to go to school.

I was not happy, and my belly was still upset. When the bus approached the house, the pain in my stomach worsened. I started crying intensely and told my mother that I didn't feel well. She gave in and said I could stay home. The bus drove off, and I was relieved. I wouldn't have to go to school feeling so awful.

Except I didn't feel so awful. I noticed this with astonishment. Once I was home free, the intense pain in my stomach eased back to the mild discomfort from before. I was confused. I had not faked any of it, including the flare-up of pain when I thought I had to go to school. My mind had created an actual physical sensation, and I had been fooled.

I realized that my body and brain had conspired to keep me home. And why? I acknowledged that something at school was bothering me quite a bit. There were two boys in this new school who were sexually assaulting the girls. At any moment, we could feel an unwanted hand—anywhere. This occurred in a crowd, in the hall, and even under the desk in class. Nowhere was safe.

At age eleven, I hadn't heard of psychosomatic (mind-body) symptoms, but I had resolved never to let my brain fool me by faking sick again. I did not like fear making my decisions for me. With this new awareness, I decided on a different strategy to deal with the problem at school.

As you can see, the brain is creative, powerful, and persuasive in its attempts to avoid uncomfortable things. To make the strategies work, the brain often hides those bad things in the subconscious where we won't have to see them.

Whether it's an anxiety-provoking situation or deep sadness, we simply don't like to feel bad, and our minds want to help. Yet when we swallow discomfort, it doesn't go away. The more we swallow and stuff the feelings down, the worse our emotional lives will become as those suppressed feelings pile up.

We must learn not to swallow our feelings. To swallow is to accumulate pain.

If you do this, don't feel bad. Swallowing is a typical response. Even therapists have the impulse to avoid. It's human. Remember the hand jerking back from a hot stove? This is us. My time with a therapist named Kelly is a good example:

Kelly volunteered at a therapeutic mindfulness workshop. She is a well-functioning, professional woman who knows how to keep her emotions in check when needed.

Kelly shared a recurring situation at work in which she had to be calm in the moment although she had a very strong emotional reaction. I guided Kelly through the process of therapeutic mindfulness, and she noticed her neck getting very hot.

I had her sit with it. When I checked in, she reported a slight reduction in emotion. I had expected a bigger change. When I asked, she acknowledged that she was trying to calm the feeling down. I suggested that instead, she allow the anxiety to be there and allow herself to notice all of it.

When I checked in with her again, the feeling had gotten bigger. I continued prompting Kelly with allowing phrases to help her not resist the emotions. After a while, I noticed a shift in her expression and asked what was happening. She shared feeling calm. I had her sit with the calm feelings in her body for a few moments, and then we discussed her experience in front of the group.

Kelly shared that the feeling had gotten so intense, it had occupied her entire chest and moved up her neck, creating a suffocating sensation. Yet as she kept allowing the process to happen, the feeling calmed completely.

I explained that the habit of pushing down the feeling just meant that she and the feeling were fighting each other. Once she allowed it to come up all the way, her mind was able to resolve this persistent issue.

The entire process took fourteen minutes.

We must allow the feelings to come up, or they never resolve. Trying to "skip ahead" is something I see often. Kelly knew that the ultimate goal of the exercise was to feel better, so she tried to skip the discomfort and jump to the part where it was all better. This is another trick of avoidance. We cannot skip the work and reap the result.

We cannot skip the work and reap the result.

Whenever we're tempted to shove our feelings into a dark corner, we must remember that we do not heal in the dark. By accepting and allowing her fear to come into the light, Kelly learned on a deep level that the feared thing was not too much for her to bear. She was able to feel the anxiety and finally know that she was safe in the present.

When we swallow emotion, the effect goes deeper than we realize. We give our minds the subconscious message that we can't handle emotion, that life is overwhelming, and ultimately, that we need to run and hide from hard things.

If we don't catch our avoidance patterns, they will grow in power. There are so many ways to avoid what we feel. For some, avoidance looks like pleasure seeking. Chasing money, sex, thrills, alcohol, and drugs or obsessively seeking approval are forms of this. For others, distractions are the preferred methods of avoidance. Playing video games, binging TV, becoming a workaholic, hyper-focusing on accomplishing more and more, or becoming consumed with other people's problems are all ways to distract ourselves from our mental world.

Keep in mind that many of these pursuits or pleasures are fine. A good Netflix binge can be great for entertainment and bonding time. However, when an activity is used for avoidance, it becomes a problem.

Some forms of avoidance seem positive. Climbing the corporate ladder gets us public accolades. One client told me when life got tough, she would respond by getting another degree. One way to check for avoidance in a very busy person is to see what happens when they stop their activities to be present with their thoughts and feelings. (This hit many people hard during the first year of the coronavirus pandemic.)

Some people look at everyone else's problems and try to fix them, save them, to do everything for them. This can be done to the exclusion of their own problems. I've known many people who thought they were being selfless, but when they spent time with themselves, they were overwhelmed with anxiety. They couldn't handle the discomfort of their own thoughts. The moment they slowed down, the urge to do absolutely anything else—*to save anyone else*—re-emerged with a vengeance.

If you relate to any of this, don't beat yourself up. Remember, we are doing the best we can with what we've learned. Most people have a limited understanding of how to be happy. In an effort to help us, they might have told us things like: "Chin up, stiff upper lip!" or, "There's no use crying over spilled milk!" or, "Just move on. You can't change it now." These attempts to control (or obliterate!) our feelings are often people's best methods of emotional survival.

The swallowing strategy even sneaks into therapy. People have come to me asking for better "coping skills," hoping I could teach them more effective ways to suppress the emotions that were adding up and becoming stronger. Although it might be hard to hear that we should face the feelings, some people were glad when I told them I could teach them how to do this.

Swallowing is good for short-term coping but can be very damaging long-term. There are plenty of sources for learning short-term coping skills. I want to teach healing. When it comes to feeling bad, the only way out is through. That means going through the emotions.

Thankfully, we do have choices. We can follow the script and swallow our feelings, or we can learn a new way. Instead of avoiding, we can learn to feel bad in a healthy way, so we can soon feel better. Always remember that bad feelings provide information about what needs to be healed inside us. They can lead us to a better life! So what other options do we have?

Strategy 2 – Wallow

> Intelligence will be used in the service of the
> neurosis.
> —Sigmund Freud

"I don't have a problem feeling my feelings!" a client declared. Indeed, she had periods of time when she did nothing but feel her feelings. When depression hit hard, she would call out of work, stay in bed, and feel sad, sometimes for days.

The problem she had, which most of us have, is that she didn't know how to feel her feelings in a way that did her any good. Instead, she went with the brain's other default strategy: she would wallow. This means she would think depressing thoughts and feel depressed for days, weeks, or even months at a time. Many, many months.

Wallowing refers to people stewing in their jerk brain thoughts. This client's depression did not go away because the story her jerk brain told her fed the depression. She would ruminate on a breakup or a lost friendship or conflicts with her parents, and her brain would tell her all the reasons she was stupid, unlikeable, and weird. She would replay social interactions and list all the made-up proof of her jerk brain's story. This brought her to the conclusion that she would be alone forever, and voilà, the depression deepened.

Jerk brain loves this strategy. When you're upset, observe your thinking. There is a pattern. Notice that each and every jerk brain thought has one purpose only: to tell you why you should be upset.

Think of your emotions as a fire and your thoughts as logs. Jerk brain loves to feed the fire! This pyromaniac has all the fuel it needs to keep that blaze going. If you're angry, it justifies your anger. If you're sad, it justifies your sadness. If you're worried, it plays endless scenarios to justify your worry. "Not only are you right to be upset," jerk brain says, "but you should be *even more upset!*" You're underestimating the situation! If you let it, jerk brain will happily help you become more upset.

Here are some generic jerk brain wallowing patterns.

Anger: "I can't believe they did that to me. It just shows how insensitive they are. They know that kind of thing bothers me. If they cared about me at all, they would have never done that. Come to think of it, I can see how they planned this out. It was on purpose! How did I never notice before how manipulative they are? I see now how they tricked me! I was a victim, and they took complete advantage. Now that I think about it, they've done this before. Clearly, they were just pretending to be nice yesterday, but it was fake. They lured me in and I'm the big sucker. They are horrible, cruel, nasty people. They can't be trusted. Come to think of it, most people can't be trusted. This is just like the time when . . ."

Depression: "I can't blame them for acting that way, really. Didn't I deserve it? If I weren't such a loser, they wouldn't treat me this way. I certainly didn't behave the best in the past. If I were a better friend, a kinder person, more helpful, more interesting, or more fun, they would value me and this would have never happened. In fact, this kind of thing has always happened to me. It's come up in other relationships too. Clearly, something's wrong with me. I'm the common denominator. In spite of everything I've tried to fix my broken self, this is still happening. Nothing is working! I'm hopeless. No one wants to be around someone like me. I'll always be alone."

Anxiety: "For years I've wanted this (job, health, romantic partner, etc.). Now that I have it, I'm hanging by a thread. There are so many ways I could lose it. I just have to think of everything that could go wrong. If I work hard enough, if I do everything perfectly and do not make any mistakes, I can avoid disaster. I'll be better, think of everything, research, plan, work hard. But what if I miss something? What if I don't plan enough? I need to stay on my toes, control all the details. I need to stop that person from getting in the way. I can't let someone else ruin everything for me! I will have to control them. If I work hard enough, I can keep everyone and everything safe, in place, as it should be. But what if I can't? There's too much pressure. I'm already cracking. Oh God, what if someone sees that I can't take it? Clearly, I can't handle everything. I'm so freaked out thinking that I'll fail . . ."

Perhaps these scenarios get you thinking about similar thought patterns you or a distressed friend has struggled with. They feel so real when we're caught up in them, but they are not unique, nor are they facts. They are standard ways our jerk brain winds us up.

John's story illustrates what can happen when we let jerk brain run our life:

John came to see me for anxiety. He had recently retired after a successful career. As the boss of a large company, John had lived a life where he needed to be in charge. He was good at this—at work and at home. He was good with money, with people, and in leadership. In spite of his busy lifestyle, he and his wife had remained close. Both had hoped retirement would be a special time in their lives.

Unfortunately, free time had only fueled John's worry habits. He mentioned having been "a worrier" since childhood. Before retirement, he could act on most of his worries, but with his children grown and no office to visit, John got stuck in his thoughts. He would lose hours not realizing he was staring off into space as his brain churned. He worried for the well-being of everyone: his children, his former employees, even friends and acquaintances. He second-guessed past decisions and was also preoccupied with making social mistakes. Whether in his volunteer work or when running into a friend, he practiced the interaction beforehand and then analyzed it afterward.

John was a wallower. His mind explored, examined, and second-guessed until he was worn out. When he read self-help books, he would use them to scrutinize his behavior and berate himself. He was stuck in insecurity about every decision he made in the past and in the present.

It took some practice before John could interrupt his thought processes. To change this lifelong habit was no small feat, but with some guidance, he was able to use a combination of new habits to take back his life. By the end of his therapy, his wife told him, "I got my husband back."

John's story illustrates how you can be successful, well-liked, and kind-hearted yet have your emotional life hijacked by jerk brain's stories. John had great relationships, yet his ongoing worries made it impossible for him to enjoy retirement. Getting away from wallowing was key for John. When you wallow, jerk brain thrives. John needed to break this habit to regain his life.

When you wallow, jerk brain thrives.

Wallowing strengthens judgment and reactivity. Therapeutic mindfulness trains us in nonjudgment.

Consider how much of your previous day involved thoughts that fed negative emotions. Reflect on your thoughts over the last hour. Were you surprised to find negative thoughts? If so, don't worry. This doesn't make you bad. Negative thoughts come automatically. Wallowing makes them worse. Wallowing pulls you into *believing* the thoughts, and that is what gives jerk brain its real power. When given the chance, such thoughts will consume your emotional life.

Having a thought doesn't make it true. You are not your thoughts, but believing a thought will make it true for you.

What do we do with this information? We have been told we need to face our feelings. Yet when we try to do just that and jerk brain takes over, we feel worse. So we push our feelings away, and we're back to the swallow strategy. It seems like a catch 22: if thinking about it and not thinking about it are both bad, what options do we have? We try our best to "get over it," "let go," or "move on." If we explore a situation and find any discomfort, then we have not moved on. Instead, it means we are swallowing again. How frustrating!

I say start with a deep breath and be gentle with yourself. Don't worry if you don't have it figured out. Neither did I. Neither do most people. So be kind in your thoughts and get ready to try something new.

Strategy 3 – Allow

Ah, *allow*. This is one of my very favorite words in the English language. Understood and applied correctly, it is the gateway to wisdom and peace.

When negative emotions blaze like a bonfire, there is another option. Rather than smothering the fire or feeding it logs, we can sit calmly and watch the fire. We can allow it to burn. With patience, the fire will die down, and eventually, the fire will go out.

Now, I know the idea of sitting and watching your emotions might sound frightening. We imagine the emotional fire will grow, engulf us, burn us up, and turn our lives to ash. But know this: the fire can only grow if we feed it.

We must allow ourselves to experience our feelings fully and without judgment. When we do, our mind has an incredible capacity for healing. And when we're done, healing doesn't just take us to a place of being "normal" or as we were. Through healing, we become wiser and more compassionate.

To allow, we go to the body. Why feel emotions in our body? There are a few reasons. First, that is where your emotions hang out. Remember how the body keeps the score. We already feel emotions in our body. That is where we start.

Second, this is a trick most people don't ever learn and one thing that makes therapeutic mindfulness different: focusing on emotions in the body enables us to stop the jerk brain story! This means we can do emotional work without being sidetracked so easily.

Third, your body can express new emotions as well as subconscious wounds from long ago. When emotions seem far bigger than the current situation, it's because they are cumulative. Often we think we've "moved past it" when we've merely tried to ignore it because we needed a way to continue with life. However, our body remembers those unhealed spots of emotional pain, so working on the current emotion can help the old wounds.

And finally, why feel emotions in your body? Quite simply, it works. When done the right way, it heals. The more we feel, without judgment, the more we let go. Or rather, the more those feelings let go of us.

True mindfulness requires nonjudgmental, focused attention. These two descriptors are the twin pillars of healing. Consider how you nurture a young child who is extremely upset. You give them your full attention and presence without judging them. You don't evaluate whether their reasons for being upset are worthy or tell them to stop crying and get over it. Think of a three-year-old who fell and scraped his knee. You simply be with him until the tears fade. Your attention is focused on his needs. Soon he's ready to run and play again.

We can use this compassion with ourselves, and we start by getting out of our thoughts and into our bodies.

So, the second pillar of healing is *nonjudgment*. In any healing method by a therapist or other healer, intense judgment (such as shame) will block healing.

When we judge, we are not accepting something. When I talk about accepting a tough situation, someone might tell me in an agitated tone, "Of course, I've accepted it. I know I can't do anything about it!"

However, acceptance is not the same as resignation. It means accepting on an emotional level rather than fighting against the inevitable with every fiber of your being. Much of this book describes ways to help you remove yourself from judgment or shift perspective on your judgments to make healing possible. In a strange irony, when we truly accept a situation emotionally, clarity comes, and we are more likely to see options for change when possible.

As you read on, keep in mind that this book discusses internal processes of healing. Allowing does not mean allowing your feelings to take over, permitting you to act them out in the world. For example, I can allow myself to be with anger to work on healing, but punching someone in a fit of temper is not acceptable within my value system.

Allowing emotions such as anger to express *in your body* will help you meet them without judgment. This can dissolve and heal them. Learning to observe feelings and inner experiences *without judgment* takes us from "wallow" to "allow."

When practicing therapeutic mindfulness, we can learn to bypass our judgments and separate ourselves from the stories that keep us in pain. As we accept our feelings, we learn to accept ourselves. We develop self-compassion and wisdom.

Therapeutic mindfulness is not some fuzzy-wuzzy, emo, silly, mushy, hippie frou-frou idea. This is a very practical solution that gets results.

Chapter Four

Mindfulness Versus Therapeutic Mindfulness

The Misuse of Mindfulness Practices

Mindfulness: The very word fills the self-help aisles at the bookstore, mindfulness apps are advertised when you play Scrabble on your phone, the idea has made its way into our business literature, our gyms, and our education system, and *Time* magazine has published multiple special editions dedicated to the science behind it. In short, mindfulness has arrived in Western civilization.

If mindfulness is everywhere, why write another book?

Well, while ideas about mindfulness are now widespread, they are often misunderstood and sometimes misused.

This is not surprising. In the East, mindfulness practices have been studied, analyzed, and practiced for thousands of years. In the West, our understanding is in its infancy. Although most people have heard of it by now, few have done the work to understand it on more than a surface level.

For purposes of this discussion, when I refer to *mindfulness practices*, that includes several practices that have elements of mindfulness. These include:

- Meditation

- Guided visualization

- Grounding

- Some coping skills (as in dialectical behavior therapy)

- Body scans

- Here-and-now mindfulness using the five senses

As people try these practices for the first time, many are impressed by the calming results. However, they often don't realize how the same exercises can become a new method of avoidance.

When I was an intern, we were all taught that we should help clients practice coping skills in each session. These skills often pull from mindfulness principles. This is how I know that some new therapists are taught mindfulness tools without any additional context or information. At the time, I did not know how such practices could be used to suppress emotions while the person thinks they're doing something good for their mental health.

Years before I developed therapeutic mindfulness, I helped a client visualize a *safe place*, a common and useful therapy practice. This client was amazed by the peacefulness she experienced, which was such a drastic departure from her typically reactive, traumatized mind. She was so relieved, in fact, that she began using it on her own. Unfortunately, she was so prone to avoiding uncomfortable emotions that whenever she started to feel bad, she would use the safe place practice to soothe herself. She never returned to work through the hard feelings she was avoiding. Even during therapy, she found such feelings almost intolerable.

One year later, her safe place stopped working. Frightening ideas and feelings intruded during her visualization, shattering her ability to use the tool at all. Since then, it has been a slow journey working on emotional tolerance.

Shortly after this incident, a new client called and described the same phenomenon. This time, I knew exactly what was happening. I took on this client and confirmed that she, too, was trying to squash down uncomfortable emotions with meditations as well as various breathing and sensory exercises.

Your mind is not stupid. It knows when you are taking a break and when you are avoiding altogether. It will give you some time to face things, but if those feelings build up too much, they will come out, like it or not. Pain is like a pressure cooker—and it's not pretty when it blows up.

This is why I differentiate between coping skills and healing skills. Coping skills are a great short-term solution. If I'm about to cry in a grocery store, I can use coping skills to get my tasks done while appearing normal. If I'm angry, I can use coping skills rather than drive dangerously. Another good time for coping skills is if I feel like crying but need to provide a young child with emotional support instead.

Later, when the groceries are purchased, I'm safely home, and the child is in bed, it is time to return to the moment I felt triggered and work through the pain that came up. Now I can use healing skills to do the deeper work.

There is a difference between avoiding and taking a break. When doing emotional work, there might be a time when you realize you are exhausted and need a break. Even with the best therapy, big feelings can take several sessions before you feel relief. In between sessions, it's okay to not stay focused on your pain all day long, every day. We can set this stuff on the shelf, so to speak. This lets us function in life.

Taking a break is fine, so long as we return to our problems soon. Having a regular time to do deep work is another good strategy, but make sure you don't pretend you'll come back to it when you continue to procrastinate. Remember the cautionary tales of the meditators above? The brain is not fooled. Finding reasons not to work on your feelings means you're back to the swallow strategy.

If you reflect and find that you've been avoiding, don't beat yourself up. Just catch it and correct the issue. Once you notice avoidance, you can always choose again. As you work on any practice to improve your mental state, the mind's tricks of avoidance will pop up. This is okay. The goal is not to be perfect—it is to learn and grow.

Becoming comfortable with being uncomfortable takes practice. It is possible to practice enough that the urge to avoid becomes negligible. This happens as you experience again and again that you can be with difficult feelings and come out the other side feeling better and stronger.

Practice and experience the effects for yourself.

What is Mindfulness?

I define mindfulness as ***nonjudgmental, focused attention***.

Meditations typically begin with exercises to focus the attention without judgment. If you've tried guided meditation, you likely have been directed to focus on your body in some way. One common way is to notice your breath with meticulous detail. For example, you might be guided to notice the temperature of the breath on your upper lip, to feel your chest rise and fall, or to imagine the muscles releasing naturally as you breathe.

Mindfulness exercises are often taught using the senses. It is noticing and describing, without judgment, what you see, hear, smell, taste, and feel with your body. It's possible to do many things either mindlessly or mindfully. You can mindfully take a walk, fold clothes or sip tea. Mindfulness is not just being aware, as many think. It is being completely focused on one thing without judgment.

Why Practice Mindfulness?

Since mindfulness practices started becoming popular in the West, scientists have studied brain scans of meditating monks, fascinated by the unusual brain activity as well as the monks' mastery over their minds and bodies.

Your brain works similarly to the way muscles work. When you exercise, you build muscle. Squats build more muscle in your thighs. Pushups build more muscle in your arms, chest, and core. In the same way, if you have practiced fearful or angry knee-jerk reactions for years, you have been building brain tissue in the areas of the brain that respond with fear or anger. When you "exercise" the part of your brain that is for relaxing, you build more brain tissue for relaxation.

Mindfulness practices go further than teaching relaxation. Over time when people practice observing without judgment, they become able to watch their jerk brain thoughts more dispassionately. When jerk brain starts ranting, they can decide how to react. They now have space to use the tools they've learned. This is one of many benefits I hear from my clients.

The good news is that you can train your brain to have calmer reactions. You can develop impulse control—the ability to pause before reacting. You can develop the ability to calm your mind and body. You can develop compassion, calmness, loving detachment, and nonjudgment.

Mindfulness practices can help develop these brain habits and skills. It is a muscle for noticing and being. It counteracts the habit of avoiding. Because it is without judgment, mindfulness also counteracts the habit of reacting. Can you see a place in your life where it would be helpful to pause and calmly consider a response versus going with your first impulse? Mindfulness teaches us how to "be." Eventually, we learn how to "be okay" whether events around us are chaotic or calm.

What is Therapeutic Mindfulness?

Therapeutic mindfulness is a step-by-step process that combines Eastern mindfulness practices with trauma-informed therapy techniques to heal feelings rather than run away from them. It can be used by people who have no prior mind training. Because some people can do this process on their own, therapeutic mindfulness is the primary tool that allows my clients to no longer need my services.

You can use therapeutic mindfulness on anger, fear, sadness, disappointment, anxiety, hurt, and emptiness. You can also use it to appreciate the positive emotions that replace the hurt ones.

Practicing therapeutic mindfulness can teach you to do the following:

- Create a habit of pausing before reacting

- Observe your reactions from a separate part of your mind that has wisdom

- Gain deep awareness of your body's expression of feelings, both negative and positive

- Learn to sit with and heal strong spikes of emotion in a short period of time

- Learn to sit with and heal old, long-held emotional reactions over time as part of your meditation practice

- Develop a deep sense of compassion and gentleness toward your own suffering and the suffering of others

Let's look at the process that creates such wonderful benefits.

CHAPTER FIVE

HOW TO PRACTICE THERAPEUTIC MINDFULNESS

We can do hard things.
—Glennon Doyle

First, a Warning:

W hile most people who function in society can handle this work, a warning here is necessary: there are people for whom professional support might be needed when beginning such a practice. One must be able to handle some emotional discomfort. There are people whose minds have developed the ability to disconnect to such an extent that they are not in touch with reality. This ability was once a survival tool for them, and it is called "dissociation." To do therapeutic mindfulness, it's important to be able to safely stay present in the body. If you dissociate, the best course might be to get a therapist who can guide this process slowly and safely.

Beware if you have experienced any of the following:

- Felt disconnected from your body, as if being outside looking at yourself

- Become spacey or dizzy when something upsetting came up

- Lost parts of your memory/blocked things out

- Felt like current situations seemed to be happening to someone else

- Felt like you were in someone else's body

- Had times when people seemed far away or unclear as if you were seeing through a fog

- Felt as though the things around you were not real

- Recalled a past event so intensely that you felt it was actually happening again

- Been somewhere but didn't recall how you got there

- Been able to ignore or been unable to feel things that would normally be painful, like a burn or a cut

- Spent extended periods of time thinking of nothing

- Lost connection with reality

Disconnecting from our body or sense of self is one of many defense mechanisms our mind has created to survive terrible emotional pain. If you experience these types of symptoms, seek a professional and share the symptoms as well as the work you're trying to do. If you cannot stay present, a skilled therapist can help you learn to touch upon your intense feelings and then bring yourself back into the present moment as needed. The therapist you seek should specialize in trauma and be knowledgeable about dissociation.

Use your discernment about whether you would like to have a therapist available when you begin this work. This is especially important if you have a trauma history that feels overwhelming. With therapeutic support, you could try therapeutic mindfulness on less intense feelings or present-day reactions. If something more intense is triggered, you can work with your trauma therapist. Keep your therapist informed about the work you do at home until you feel stable and secure. Practicing therapeutic mindfulness can help you develop the ability to tolerate more difficult emotions, which can then aid your healing work in therapy.

The Process – Step by Step

This is the moment we've been waiting for! Here is the process for therapeutic mindfulness:

Step 1. Choose – a target.

Step 2. Describe – your body reactions.

Step 3. Allow – practice nonjudgment.

Step 4. Repeat – steps 2 and 3 until the feeling is gone.

Step 5. Return – to the target.

Let's look at this process more closely.

Step 1. Choose a Target

Therapeutic mindfulness uses a form of mindfulness meditation to work specifically on negative emotions. The first step is to choose a target. What painful thing would you like to no longer be in pain about?

Characteristics of a good target:

1. It is specific. It is an image or thought that you can pinpoint.

2. It is charged with emotion. When you pay attention to this target, you should feel an emotional reaction.

The image can be a memory that bothers you or an imagined event that bothers you. A scene from the past (i.e., hiding in your closet when mom and dad fought) or the future (i.e., your spouse suggesting divorce) is the target. It can be an image of repeated events (i.e., you taking care of your siblings while mom is passed out on the couch). It can be present events that bother you (i.e., a recurring fight with a spouse or an interaction at work that gets under your skin). Once you connect to strong emotion, then you've got your target and you can skip to step 2.

Because of the mind's tendency to swallow, you might not have strong emotions immediately for a memory you know is problematic. Thinking of the details can bring up emotions. Try to imagine the things you would see, hear, or smell. Ask yourself what the worst part of the image is and focus on that.

Once you become aware of the emotion getting stronger, freeze the image. Think of it like hitting Pause on a movie. Look at the worst part. That's your target.

Sometimes the target is a thought. For example, if you're thinking about a series of memories and have the thought, "She never really loved me," followed by a wave of emotion, pause there. The thought, "She never really loved me," is your target.

If you have too many things jumping out as targets and they are overwhelming your senses, just pick one. If it is an image, hit Pause on the movie. You can even choose one part of the scene to look at. For example, if an object within a memory brings up strong emotion, then do therapeutic mindfulness while focusing on that object until it feels neutral or calm. Then hit Play on the movie to check whether other parts of the memory hold strong emotion.

The same goes for thoughts: If a barrage of intensely emotional thoughts hits you, simply pick one and find what it brings up in the body. Do therapeutic mindfulness on that until it feels neutral or calm. Then you can move on to the next thought. *Core beliefs* also make great targets. You'll read more about *core beliefs* in chapter 10.

Once you have a strong reaction, you might feel resistance. You might want to run. If so, you've hit upon something important. Remember, feelings give you information. If you are emotionally able, this is exactly the time to lean in.

To summarize: If it hurts, that is your target. If you really want to avoid it, then it is definitely your target. It's time for step 2.

Note: When choosing to do work on yourself, you can pick a target for your work. One purpose of the target is to activate the emotional reaction you wish to heal. If you are already very emotional at any moment, you can go straight to step 2 and get into your body.

Step 2. Describe – Your Body Reactions

The first key to doing therapeutic mindfulness is to get out of your jerk brain's story and focus on your body. If you're thinking, "Okay, but how?" this is where it gets interesting because step 2 is the answer.

Hopefully, you've been practicing exercise 3 from chapter 2, checking in with your body. Now we're going to go deeper. You can start with these questions:

- What are you feeling? You can name an emotion here: sadness, anger, anxiety, fear, or hurt.

- Where is it in your body?

If it is hard to find or feels like it is everywhere, you can ask yourself these questions:
- If it were one place in my body the most, where would it be?

- If it were somewhere in my body, where would it be?

For example, most people don't have strong emotions in their toes! When someone says it's "everywhere," it can help them to compare the feeling in their toes to the feeling in their chest, stomach, or throat. Often the answer becomes clear. If it's equally strong in two places, such as in the head and chest, I simply have them choose one. There is no wrong answer.

Note that it is possible to feel emotions in your head. This is not the same as having thoughts in your head. People have reported head sensations such as pressure or heaviness.

Emotions in the body take on a very physical form during this exercise. Describe the feeling in detail. These questions will get you focused on your body and give you a more vivid awareness of the physical feeling.

Imagine the feeling is a separate physical thing and ask yourself the following:
- If it had a size, how big would it be? (The feeling might be in your body but could also feel as big as a house.)

- If it had a shape, what would that be? (A ball or a brick is common, although I've heard more unusual things like a ginger root or a blade.)

- If it had a weight, how heavy would it feel?

- If it had a temperature, what would that feel like? (Sometimes people have a very strong sense of hot or cold.)

- If it had a color, what would that be?

- If it had a texture, what would it feel like to the touch? (This often leads to answers about the outside texture such as rough, smooth, or spiky. I sometimes also ask: Is it dense or hard? Sometimes the feeling is dense, sometimes empty or hollow, and sometimes sticky or spongy. There are no wrong answers.)

- If it had a sound, what would that be like? (I don't ask this one often, but on occasion it is a powerful aspect of the feeling.)

- Is there movement to the feeling? Or is it stuck in place? Describe what you notice.

I sometimes ask about sound and movement, but often by the time I get to texture, the feeling has become vivid enough to have the person focused on it and no longer in their story. This is the goal.

When describing the feeling in the body, go with your instincts. While it is unlikely that there is *literally* a dark blue and green ball of sticky, heavy goo sloshing about in your stomach or a black cloud of pressure pushing against the inside of your skull, just go with it. As you ask the questions, your mind will often have an answer for you, even if it doesn't make sense to your logical brain.

Your mind expresses in symbols, not in words. Remember, we are going deeper into the mind than talk therapy, and your abstract impressions might surprise you. Keep going. By asking the questions, you may find that your impressions of the feeling become more vivid.

If you search and sense there is no answer to a specific question, don't worry about it. Move to the next question. For example, I'll have a client struggle with how horribly cold the feeling is. The next client won't sense a temperature at all. This is fine. Simply describe any impressions that come up and move on to the next question.

To make step 2 simple, use the "Body Focusing Questions" handout (see the Appendix). If it helps you to visualize, have someone read the questions to you, or record yourself asking the questions and giving time for answers. This way you can close your eyes and focus on the process.

This step enables you to face feelings without wallowing! Once you are out of your thoughts and fully focused on the physical feeling in your body, it's time to go to step 3.

Step 3. Allow – Practice Nonjudgment

Allow—my favorite part! This is where the magic happens.

Now that you're focused on an uncomfortable physical feeling, the next step is to *allow it to be there*. You will do this using *allowing phrases* that help you get into a mindset of nonjudgment.

After describing the feeling in detail, you might be very uncomfortable. At least part of you might be pushing against having the feeling. For example, you might notice that the feeling is tight, heavy, hot, nauseous, achy, and uncomfortable and you don't like it! It is not intuitive to lean into discomfort in such an intimate way, but that is exactly what needs to happen at this point. One of the best phrases to remember is, "Let yourself be uncomfortable."

The concept of letting yourself be uncomfortable is a game changer. It takes the judgment out of the process and puts you in a place of observing the discomfort instead.

You can use this or other allowing phrases to get you into an observational headspace. For example, I might prompt a client to go from step 2 to step 3 by saying the following:

> "Okay, the feeling is like a fist squeezing your throat. It's red and very hot, hard like stone and heavy. Keep noticing that. Notice how big that hand feels. Notice your body tensing in response to the feeling. Now, this might sound strange, but I want you to allow it to be there. Give it space. It is uncomfortable, but see if you can let yourself be uncomfortable, just for now."

While watching the feeling in the body, I use allowing phrases like, "Just notice," and, "Let yourself be uncomfortable, just for now," and "Your only job is to observe."

Even when I'm doing this on my own, I still have the subconscious impulse to resist discomfort. I have to remind myself by saying in words, "Let it be there."

The physical feeling is a part of us. Our mind is expressing something in us that is hurt. To push it away is to tell ourselves that we are stupid or weak for having feelings or that we are unworthy of care. To push it away is to tell ourselves that part of us is unacceptable and we must shove it into a dark corner where no one can see it. To push it away is to say our feelings are too much—that *we* are too much. Can you see how this impulse is a way of being harsh in our time of need?

Yet if someone we love and don't judge, like a young child, came to us crying or scared, a nurturing response would not be to push the feeling away. Even if we can't fix it, we still comfort the child by staying with them. As we give the child all our caring attention, the child starts to calm down. There is deep comfort in receiving focused attention with compassion and without judgment. It is like being truly accepted.

This is what we're doing when we allow the feeling to show up completely in our body. We sit with the part of ourselves that is hurt. We give it all of our attention without telling it to go away. Allowing feelings to be there is a deeply kind thing to do. For some, it might be the first time they've ever felt truly heard.

As we stay with the feeling and it improves, we come to realize that we aren't too much. For many of us, we need to experience that we can be with a feeling and that it will not break us.

If you've ever heard people say we need to love ourselves and wondered, "Sure, but how?" this is your answer. This process teaches us how to stay and nurture the parts of ourselves that show up in childlike pain. Instead of beating ourselves up, we pause and listen.

Chapter 9 provides perspectives to increase self-compassion, but you can start with the "Allowing Phrases" handout (see the Appendix). These phrases help us drop our judgments and allow the healing process to flow.

Step 4. Repeat – Steps 2 and 3 Until the Feeling Is Gone

Steps 2 (Describe) and 3 (Allow) are recursive processes that continue until the feeling is gone, or until you run out of time for your practice.

You found a target, felt it in your body, and then told yourself to allow it to be there. Perhaps the feeling got bigger or smaller or moved to another location. Perhaps the temperature or texture became more comfortable. In order to stay focused, describe the changes in sensation. The impressions of the feelings tend to change. The emotion might be less hot and spiky. Or instead of red, it is now blue. Continue step 2 by describing the feeling in your body.

Once you've been watching the feeling and noticing the changes in this way, then return to step 3 using the allowing phrases ("Just notice," "Let yourself be uncomfortable, just for now," and, "Your only job is to observe.") and remind yourself to allow the feeling to shift and change in whatever way it needs. Your only job is to observe what your body is experiencing.

I like to think of the entire process as visualized in diagram 1.

Diagram 1.

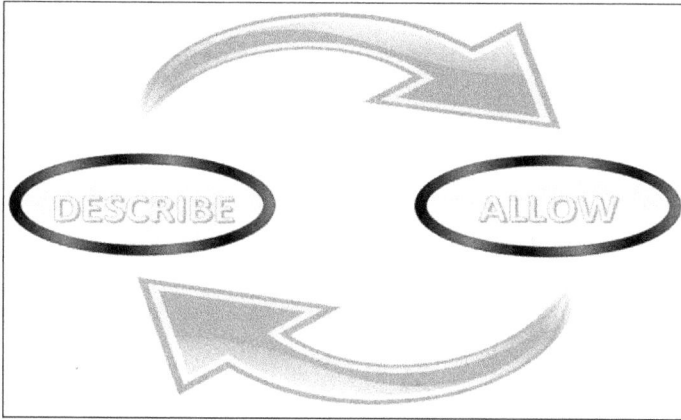

Therapeutic mindfulness feels difficult at times, but the process is a simple one. Just continue to describe the shifting sensations and then remind yourself to flow with them. To describe, it helps to use modified body-focusing questions like the following:

- Describe the feeling now. (This open question allows for unusual impressions to arise.)

- Is it getting better or worse?

- Is it bigger or smaller?

- Is it heavier or lighter?

- Is it darker or lighter? What is the color?

- What does the temperature feel like now?

- Is it getting tighter or easing up?

- Is it moving?

I look for changes where a person had a vivid response. If they noticed a lot of movement, such as swirling in the stomach, I will ask if the movement is faster or slower. If they describe something very specific, such as a ball with sharp spikes, I ask how sharp the spikes feel. I often ask about size, color, and temperature.

This process continues by describing the physical feeling, then reusing your favorite allowing phrases to help you drop resistance and lean into the feeling.

The initial wave of emotion usually becomes tolerable within moments once a person drops the resistance and allows. After the initial improvement, the emotion is usually less intense but present. When this happens, I strongly advise you to continue. The goal, after all, is to heal the feeling. When possible, continue with the process until the negative feeling is gone completely or is barely detectable. I've seen many targets cleared in less than thirty minutes. You can even continue focusing on your body by Describing and enjoying the feeling of relief and lightness that comes afterward.

For some complicated targets, the strongest emotion will wane, and your attention will shift to a second wave of emotion that shows up differently in your body. When this happens, your mind is tempted to tell a story about what is going on. For example, say you have anxiety about speaking in front of a crowd and you feel self-conscious about being judged by the crowd. You might be working on the fear in your chest. As the feeling in your chest subsides, you have a thought, "But what if my talk isn't good enough?" Now a fist squeezes your throat and a story starts with this new focus.

When this happens, you can acknowledge the new thought, then return to therapeutic mindfulness by getting out of the story and into your body. Start with step 2 and describe the strongest feeling in your body (in this case, the squeezing fist) using the body focusing questions. Then repeat your preferred allowing phrases from step 3.

Whenever something changes during therapeutic mindfulness, simply acknowledge whatever you notice, then return to steps 2 and 3.

Therapeutic Mindfulness on Positive Emotions

As the negative feelings fade or disappear completely, you will notice pleasant feelings in place of them. These are also expressed in your body. As an optional step, you can continue your mindfulness practice on the pleasant sensations.

How do you do this? If you guessed, "Describe the feelings in your body and allow them to be there," you've got it!

You can continue therapeutic mindfulness on how you feel without the pain and deepen your positive experience. Life is not only about dealing with pain. This is an opportunity to experience a positive emotional state with full awareness.

Notice what it is like to be calm and content. You might want to close your eyes and describe how it feels in your body. Getting deep into feeling calm might be a new experience. You might notice things such as the following:

- "My chest feels open."

- "My head feels clear."

- "My breathing is deeper."

- "My shoulders are no longer heavy—they feel light."

- "My body is relaxed."

- "I feel calm, at peace."

- "My heart feels calm."

Let it sink in. Memorize the physical feelings. Notice what it is like to be in your body in this relaxed state. Enjoy it. When you end your sessions this way, you might find that you *want* to go through this process again so you can get to this feeling again.

It is powerful to learn that not only can you be with your true feelings and not crack, but that you can feel good afterward. Being in your body in a healed moment is a truly special event. Take time to savor it.

Step 5. Return – To the Target

Once you find yourself feeling calm with little or no negative emotions, check back in with the target. Remember the image or thought that began with such strong emotion? Go back to that. When you look directly at it, is there any negative feeling that comes up? This confirms whether you've done some healing.

When you look at the target, is the pain less intense than before? Is it gone completely? If the feeling has lessened, you can finish working through additional sensations until this target is clear. When the target brings up nothing, you know you've accomplished healing. Something that caused strong emotional pain thirty minutes ago is barely there or gone.

Checking back in is also a way to find out whether other negative feelings go with that target. For example, you might have worked through sadness around a memory only to return and find anger. In this case, the anger around that image or thought is your new target. You can look for the sadness and see whether that's resolved. You can also choose to begin the process on the anger—either now or in your next practice session.

To continue your practice, start at step 1 and choose another target. In this way, you can heal your hurts piece by piece.

CHAPTER SIX
WHAT TO EXPECT

Hopefully, you've become so curious and excited about this process that you've tried it out already. If so, you might have questions about what is normal and whether you are doing it right.

The first thing you should know is not to plan where the process should take you. For example, don't *try* to calm down or *try* to forgive. This journey takes different forms, and you will naturally get where you need to go as you heal. If you catch yourself doing this, remind yourself to notice what you're trying to change and allow it to be present. You can't think your way through this process. Besides, if we could heal with logic, this would be a very different book!

Your subconscious mind has great wisdom and powerful healing capabilities. Try to drop expectations about how the process should go. Even though this might be awkward, we must get out of our own way. We must allow the process to happen in just the way it needs to. Don't worry about judging the content. Your subconscious mind will steer the ship. The only thing you need to assess is whether you are judging or resisting. If you are focused on your body and open to the process, you're on the right track.

This chapter describes some experiences people have had when doing therapeutic mindfulness. The goal is to provide understanding as to when things are working and when to get more help. Sitting openly with the body's emotions is far more powerful than you know. Chances are, you are doing it just right.

What Does the Process Feel Like?

When initially learning this practice, it might feel foreign, uncomfortable, scary, and absolutely counter-intuitive. When we have intense feelings, opening up to them is not our first impulse!

Because there is a strong compulsion to stay in our story, a common first reaction I see after a person taps into the feeling is an attempt to explain it. For example, I might ask, "What do you feel and where is it in your body?" Here is a typical response: "I feel heaviness on my shoulders and neck. It's all the stress because the last time I had a boss hovering over a big project, next thing I knew . . ." and the story continues.

Or this: "I feel tightness in my chest. My heart starts pounding when I think about it. My husband was acting exactly like this a year ago before he relapsed . . ." and the story continues.

Sharing your thoughts is fine, and you can do this for the other twenty-three hours and forty minutes in the day. But when working to heal emotions, we must go past the story. At this point, I gently interrupt the story and refocus on the body. I then use the procedure outlined in the last chapter.

Some people fall into the process with no problem once they get their focus on the body. After they decide to allow discomfort, things start to change. Ideally, the hard part lasts for a few moments, and then I see my clients' faces become smoother and their breathing eases up. I know they are focused on the body and doing the work. For some, this transition begins within two minutes. For others, it's slower, but I help by repeating ideas that help with allowing or with compassion (see chapters 7 and 9).

It is common to work through a feeling in twenty or thirty minutes, although for some people, it takes longer. Some people need to keep working on a feeling again and again to help it diminish over time. Here's one client who did this intuitively:

> When I met Joanna, she didn't know how to work through her feelings. Her grief over her grandmother's death had stacked onto prior grief of loved ones who had passed. All her sadness weighed on her, resulting in random crying spells and general depression.
>
> The first time I guided Joanna to use therapeutic mindfulness on her

grief, she felt a heavy, dark boulder that weighed her down. Within the first session, the boulder became harder to find. She used the process of therapeutic mindfulness in between sessions, practicing whenever grief was triggered in different areas of her life.

After a few weeks, Joanna reported that the boulder had gotten smaller each time she practiced and that it was now a pebble. More importantly, she felt empowered to deal with grief and other strong emotions on her own.

Once Joanna got the tools to face her emotions, she ran with it. Therapeutic mindfulness quickly gave her the ability to function and not be overwhelmed by daily sadness. Soon her grief was minimal and she was able to enjoy her good memories more. This illustrates using therapeutic mindfulness to heal one issue over a period of weeks.

Experiencing a feeling becoming smaller or less intense is common. Once in a while, a person has a sense of a feeling physically leaving their body. Usually, when I check the target after this, the upsetting event or thought has no emotional charge. It is simply no longer a problem.

Remember to stay with the process for extra benefit. It is powerful to notice how the body feels without the pain and sit with it for a while, expanding our ability to pause and appreciate feeling good.

Remember also that if you get a new feeling, thought, memory, or anything else that jumps in, acknowledge the change. Then describe what comes up in your body and continue the process of describing and allowing.

What if I Notice Weird Things?

If you notice weird things, good! You're not in your logical, controlled way of thinking. It's time to roll with it. Our subconscious minds are not linear. Remember how weird dreams are? They don't explain things to us in a coherent way.

Like dreams, therapeutic mindfulness is led by the subconscious mind and therefore is abstract. People not used to working with the abstract will often describe a physical sensation and then check in with me about whether they are "doing it right." Or they might say, "It was like a heavy rock in my chest, but now it's spreading out. Is that normal?"

"It is normal?"—I've heard this so many times.

Rule of thumb: If the body sensation is changing in any way, that is a good sign! Try to stick with the process to the end. If emotions become more intense or less intense, something is changing. If the intensity stays the same but the feeling moves to a different location or turns another color, something is changing.

If you stay with the process until the feelings are ready to go away, you will start to learn how your body heals. You will gain confidence, but you must go out on a limb and try. You can only know by experiencing it for yourself.

Common experiences during therapeutic mindfulness are as follows:

- Heaviness or tightness in the chest

- Heaviness or tightness in the shoulders

- Heaviness weighing down the head

- Clenched feeling in the throat (like a fist)

- Something blocking the throat

- Tightness in the jaw

- Feeling spacey or sleepy

- Pressure or cloudiness in the head

- Pain or tears behind the eyes

- Pain in one shoulder

- Pain over the heart

- Headaches

- Stomach queasiness

- A sensation of heat or cold

- Tension in other places in the body

Less common sensations also arise. There are times when the physical feelings become strong. Sharp pain, headaches, or nausea can arise and then dissolve completely. Some people will have a strong sense of imagery, such as a hand squeezing their throat or a blade in their skull. One of my favorites was when a client described a flat disc in her chest that turned into a ginger root and then later sprouted a purple flower!

This is all normal, and the next step is always the same. Continue to describe and allow (steps 2 and 3). Your body will work through the rest.

Over time, you will become used to how your body works with emotions. Your awareness of your emotional states will grow. It will become natural to quickly notice when your body is reacting—sometimes even before you realize something is bothering you. This skill enables you to pause before things escalate.

As you continue to practice, you might even find yourself looking forward to practicing when you get emotional. This could be the weirdest thing of all! As one client explained recently, she started looking forward to it because of how good she feels afterward.

Body and Emotional Awareness

Some people need to practice connecting with emotions and being vulnerable. Spending time with a caring therapist can be useful for lessening your fear of vulnerability and shame. If you're able to connect to your body but are simply not in the habit of doing so, these short body checks can be very effective in building body awareness. (See exercise 3, chapter 2.)

How vivid or strange the process seems, differs from person to person. Here is one example of a client who had almost no body awareness and how this changed over the years with practice:

> Mark avoided feelings by working, napping, or drinking. When I first tried to get him to breathe deeply, I would demonstrate breathing slowly. When he would try to exhale, his stomach and chest would collapse in one huff. I pointed out the difference—much to his surprise. He hadn't realized he couldn't breathe deeply, even when he tried. It took several weeks working with him, but Mark's breathing improved with practice.

When we began therapeutic mindfulness, deep breathing was key for Mark because he struggled to recognize physical sensations. The first sensation he could connect to was difficulty breathing. Soon he was able to identify a sense of heaviness on his chest, like the foot of an elephant standing on him. As the heaviness lessened, his breathing opened up.

With his breath, Mark was learning slowly to be aware of his body's reactions, but he didn't connect all the dots right away. Whenever I brought up a touchy subject, Mark would yawn compulsively. He would tell me he was getting dizzy and that he needed to lie down or sleep. His expression would be normal, while tears trickled onto his cheeks. When I would mention the tears, he would touch his face to check. Initially, he insisted that everyone leaked tears while yawning.

Once I pointed out that he had talked for thirty-five minutes straight without a single yawn, yet when I mentioned a difficult subject, he yawned three times in ninety seconds. He insisted it was because he hadn't had his second cup of coffee for the day. This was typical of our early work together.

Mark continued to gain awareness of his bodily reactions. While his first sensation was usually the heaviness on his chest, he became able to accept and identify that dizziness and sleepiness were related to oncoming emotion. He sometimes felt pain behind his eyes or pressure at his temples.

With help and continued practice, Mark eventually noticed more abstract experiences when working through deep fear. In one session, Mark's overwhelming fear appeared as "a black cloud of doom." As I instructed him to allow the doom to come, it flowed into him through his head, down through his chest, and back out of his body. The longer he stayed with this, the lower the intensity became.

Mark also developed the ability to practice therapeutic mindfulness on his own on day-to-day issues. He recently shared that life gets harder when he stops doing this, and although he wants to avoid the work, he always feels better after he does it.

As you can observe in this case, someone who was not aware of his breathing or even his tears was able to work with his body until he could sense and visualize the emotions in a variety of ways, allowing him to do healing work on his own.

My own awareness of body sensations has expanded through this practice. My early attempts mostly involved the chest. Now I can quickly check in with reactions in my jaw, throat, shoulders, and sometimes stomach and head. Once, I felt a sensation like a sawblade in my skull, with pain culminating in a piercing point in my left eye. I had a flash of a related memory, and I acknowledged the memory and returned to the describe and allow procedures (steps 2 and 3). Then I sat with the pain until it subsided.

It is common to increase body awareness with practice, while some people's body communicates vividly and creatively right away. Here is an example:

It was only Grace's second time using therapeutic mindfulness. She felt a strong sense of sadness over her heart. When I asked her to describe it, she said it was like a fountain of water pouring from an endless source. I helped her accept and work through this "fountain of sadness." As it dissipated, she described a feeling like a rope tied around her rib cage, tightly holding in all her emotions. She knew the rope was a fear of feeling deeply. We focused on allowing that fear to show her how tight it needed to be and accepting the part of her that felt the need to protect herself in this way.

Grace's fear felt huge, and work on the feeling around her chest continued for several sessions. In a later session, she sensed a cage compressing her chest. The cage indicated the need to hold everything inside and locked away. We worked on this several times. Eventually, she was able to do deep work in session and on her own.

Grace was a very logical and practical person in daily life. She found these impressions quite strange, but I encouraged her to let them progress without her interference. She has since become a believer in the power of healing tapped by this process.

As you can see, each person experiences bodily sensations differently. They might be unusual and expressive or similar each time you do the work: either is normal.

Here are more examples of how feelings might show up and change. For reference, the examples are written with the body focusing questions in mind.

- Body focusing question: If the feeling was somewhere in your body, where would it be?
  Change: The feeling was in the center of my chest, but now it has moved to my throat.
  Change: The feeling was in the center of my chest, but now it is spreading out. It feels lighter.

- Body focusing question: If the feeling had a color, what would it be?
  Change: The color changed from black to dark gray.

- Body focusing question: If the feeling had a temperature, what would it be?
  Change: The feeling was hot. Now it feels room temperature.

- Body focusing question: If the feeling had a size, how big would it be?
  Change: It felt like a softball in my chest. Now it's the size of a golf ball.
  Change: It was like a softball in my chest. Now it's bigger but spreading out like a thin plate. It is less intense.

- Body focusing question: If the feeling had a weight, how heavy would it be?
  Change: It felt like fifty pounds. Now it feels like ten.
  Change: It felt like two elephant feet standing on my chest; now it feels like one.

- Body focusing question: If the feeling had a texture, what would it feel like to touch?
  Change: The feeling was spiky, but now it feels smoother, kind of bumpy.

- Body focusing question for change: Is the feeling getting better or worse/more or less intense or is it shifting?
  Change: It started as a cold ball in my chest. It got worse, the coldness was going

all the way up to my neck, filling my chest, down to my waist, and out to my arms. It was overwhelming. Then it got smaller. Now it is like the shape of a pencil in my chest, and it is no longer cold.

Know that when you begin, the feeling could get worse initially. If you're not dwelling on your thoughts, this usually means that there is suppressed emotion hiding under the surface. This is a critical moment. What should you do? If you guessed, "Describe the feelings in your body and allow them to be there," you've got it!

Even when the feeling gets more intense, the process remains the same. If you're focused in the body and without judgment, the intensity will usually be temporary.

What if you can't find anything in the body after trying all these tips?

While most people find some sensation in the body (unless they are dissociating), I've seen people struggle to feel in the body. Not everyone feels safe in their body. If they don't, the mind sometimes protects them from body sensations, and the sensations they do have stay stuck.

If you have this issue, there is something else you can try. If you are feeling very emotional, but it doesn't seem to be in your body, do the same process on the feeling as if it were an entity on its own, outside your body. This is what I did with Mary:

> Mary was visibly upset. She was sniffling and wiping tears from her eyes and said she was very sad, but she didn't feel anything in her body. I asked a few probing questions, but her chest felt open, and in spite of having tears, she said there was no pressure behind her eyes.
>
> She noticed a tight sensation in her throat and jaw, which changed a bit using therapeutic mindfulness, but not much. Also, these sensations did not feel like sadness to her. We had found them using a body scan.
>
> Since her sadness was clearly present and big, I knew we should be able to help it with therapeutic mindfulness. I told her it was okay if the sadness wasn't in her body. Instead, I asked her, "If you could imagine the sadness outside your body, how big would it be?" I said it might be as big as a house, or as big as a car, and she nodded at that statement. I continued

the body focusing questions, and she described the sadness as the size of a car, black, cold, and hard. I prompted her with allowing phrases and continued the process of describing and allowing.

As time went on, the sadness reduced to the size of a bicycle, and it became chilly instead of cold. It continued to stay black and hard and chilly, but it shrank again to the size of a baseball bat. When this happened, I knew there had been a change because I saw her face relax.

Because the sadness was related to a big, ongoing issue in her life, I asked for her instinct on whether some sadness needed to stick around or whether it might have room to get smaller. She thought it would stay the same, so I had her tell the sadness that she could come back again to listen to it. She was fine doing this.

Getting into the body might be more direct and personal, but I've mentioned how determined our mind can be about avoiding. As a plan B, visualizing the feeling as a separate thing still can yield good emotional work. Over time, the ability to be in the body could evolve, as it has for several of my clients.

Movement of Feelings

Many people feel sensations primarily in one or two places. One person feels her stomach get knotted up. Another person feels tingly in his arms and hands only. A third person feels anxiety as squeezing in the chest but feels sadness as a clutching in the throat. The primary sensations might get more or less uncomfortable or change in quality, but the feeling sticks to the same spot.

Other people's feelings act like a pinball, with emotions moving all around. This is also normal. One common scenario is movement in the trunk area. For example, a person has a feeling in the solar plexus. As they observe, it drops to the stomach. Then it goes to the throat and clenches there, then moves back to the solar plexus. It might extend, change shape, touch multiple areas, and then shrink to tightness in the chest.

When a feeling moves around, the most important thing is to *let it move*. Our job is to invite the feeling to express itself as it needs to.

In other cases, the physical sensations might take on a pulsing pattern, where they become stronger and weaker, ebb and flow. Either way, when the feeling is moving all around or doing unusual things, our response is always the same: we allow the wisdom of our minds and bodies to process emotions. We observe mindfully. Remember, *mindfully* means focused and without judgment. We do not worry that the sensation fades, then strengthens again, or that it keeps moving. We simply allow it to shift and change as it chooses.

Whether your emotions stay in one spot or move all around does not matter. Change is what you are looking for. Change generally means progress. If the pulsing gets less intense overall, it is making progress. If a feeling is in one spot but gets less hot or cold or dark during the process, this is progress.

If the intensity of emotion gets worse, you're still making progress! That is true so long as you are not feeding the emotion with jerk brain thoughts. If you are in your body (and not in your thoughts) and a feeling wants to get worse, allow it! This typically means you're getting in touch with swallowed feelings. *You can't heal what you deny, so the feelings need to come up.* Once a feeling comes up, you have an opportunity to heal something that your mind has been hiding and carrying with you.

Once you're used to the process, you might be able to do it while taking a walk, while showering, during a restroom break at an event, or in your car over lunch.

If you find you feel worse because of disturbing thoughts that come up or you find yourself getting stuck, look for information on how to move forward in chapter 8, "Basic Troubleshooting"; chapter 9, "How to Apply Non-Judgment and Self-Compassion"; and chapter 11, "Resistance."

CHAPTER SEVEN

THE MINDFUL PHRASES

By exploring what to expect in the last chapter, you can see more of what you might be describing in step 2 of therapeutic mindfulness. This chapter more deeply examines the allowing phrases to assist you with step 3. Hopefully, this will familiarize you with language that helps you be kind to yourself.

The allowing phrases discussed below help us relax the judgments that keep our hurts in place. When preparing to do therapeutic mindfulness, read through the list of allowing phrases (see the Appendix), and pick the phrase(s) that speak the most to you. You will want to repeat them as you have uncomfortable feelings come up in your body.

Below is a bit more description of the phrases to help put you in a nonjudgmental mindset. You might find it helpful to journal what comes to mind as you read these. Any key phrases or ideas that help you be gentle to yourself are worth repeating many times. These are the phrases used in step 3 of therapeutic mindfulness as described in chapter 5. The word *it* in the phrases refers to the feeling in your body.

"Allow it to be there." This is a simple but powerful reminder to let ourselves feel.

"Let it be there, just for now." I use this phrase when I sense the person I'm working with struggling with discomfort. It is a reminder that the discomfort won't last forever. It is temporary and it will pass. You might also say things like, **"This won't be forever; it's just for now."**

"Just notice." This phrase helps us connect to a mindful way of thinking. There is power when we learn to watch all inner experiences without reaction.

"Allow it space." Sometimes it is helpful to think of or visualize making room or physical space for the uncomfortable feeling.

"Open up to it." Here's another helpful phrase to help us imagine making room for the feeling to express what is needed.

"I can let myself be uncomfortable." This can help us shift our mindset from our default of wanting to avoid any discomfort. Learning to be okay with being uncomfortable, along with observing nonjudgmentally, is key to emotional growth.

"I can let myself feel all of it." This powerful phrase is meant to invite full expression of the hurt part. If this statement feels accessible, you can use it to up your therapeutic mindfulness game. There's more on this idea in chapter 13, "Therapeutic Mindfulness – Advanced."

"Notice all of it." This phrase helps us lean into discomfort, letting us dare to explore the extent of our feelings. This might be overwhelming for some, yet for those who can handle more discomfort, this invitation can help break through to the other side of emotional pain. After the breakthrough comes relief and healing.

"My only job is to observe." This is one of my favorites. It reminds us that we need not do anything with the discomfort. We do not have to fix it or change it. In fact, if we try to change the feeling, we are not accepting it as it is. We need a reminder at times that there is no need to react. We have one job: to observe whatever comes up. At times I will emphasize this idea with phrases such as: **"I don't have to fix or change anything, just observe."**

"Try to let myself feel it, just for a few minutes." This is another phrase to remind you that the discomfort is temporary, but it is also meant to imply gentleness to yourself if you are not ready to feel it for too long.

"Just be with it." A simple reminder.

"Watch it with open curiosity." I love this phrase! It encapsulates the heart of mindfulness. Open curiosity helps to drop judgment. It is a gentle way of exploring your inner experience. Note: If this phrase gets you analyzing, do not use it. The curiosity is about what the physical feeling will do next. An alternative phrase is, **"Notice how interesting it is to watch the feeling."**

"I care about this feeling." Each part of us that shows up in pain needs care. This direct statement of compassion takes it a step further. Talking to ourselves in this way is far different than what many of us habitually do, and it can change critical inner voices that we may carry. Only use this if it feels right for you. There's more on self-compassion in chapter 9.

"Notice the part of you that needs to express this and the part of you that doesn't want to feel this." Or you could say, **"Notice the part of you that needs to express this and the part of you that judges yourself for feeling this."** When you're struggling with contradictions, such as a strong feeling wanting to express itself and a strong desire to push it down, these are the types of statements that help. Rather than being frustrated with yourself, you acknowledge all aspects of your experience, then continue to describe and allow with your focus on the strongest feeling in your body.

"Remember, this is a hurt part of me that needs to be heard." This important reminder guides us to be kind to our hurt parts. I say this almost every time I guide someone, so they can get in the habit of viewing themselves with compassion. We tend to judge ourselves for not being perfectly healed already. Remember to nurture yourself as you would a young child or loved one who is hurt. Our hurt parts are often much like the child version of ourselves, stuck in a place of feeling young, vulnerable, and in pain. For more on this way of thinking, see the sections about hurt parts in chapter 9.

"Notice that I am handling this. It is not too much. I am not too much." We often fear that our emotions are too much. While many people are phobic of intense emotions, that doesn't mean that we are too much or that our feelings must be squashed. When therapeutic mindfulness is going well, this statement helps remind us that we are capable of strength in the face of difficult things.

"My job is to hang out with the feeling. That's it. There is no need to analyze—I can do that later. Just be with it." This reminds us that the purpose is not to analyze, just to be present with the emotion.

"Do not try to *make* it better. The feeling just needs to be heard." This concept is vital to the practice of therapeutic mindfulness. When we try to *make* it better, two things happen. First, we judge that what is happening is bad, because we have a need to make it go away. Now we are no longer mindful because there is judgment. Second, we are telling the feeling that it is unacceptable and telling ourselves that something about us is bad. Feelings need to be allowed to show up all the way, just as they are. Until they are accepted, they will keep pleading their case, crying their pain, screaming their anger, etcetera. When we give the feelings our complete, accepting presence and allow them to share their hurt, they can finally let go of the need to be heard. This is when they get better.

Accepting the Change Process

Accepting your experience does not mean resigning yourself to a life of hopeless despair. Accepting is not about giving up. It is also not about fighting. You can accept how things are within a process of change. You can accept who you are within a process of change. You cannot *not* change. Change will happen. The question is: Are you changing by becoming more stressed or by learning to flow with life? When we fight where we are emotionally, we become more embedded in struggle. This is because we are practicing a mindset of fighting ourselves.

Picture a woman paddling a canoe across a lake. She must accept where she is in the process in order to take the next steps and move forward. Let's say halfway through, she decides she should already be on the other side. Instead of rowing, she throws a fit and slams the oar on the water, nearly tipping the boat. In a fit of anger, she paddles furiously before realizing she has turned the boat in the wrong direction. Exasperated and exhausted, she escapes reality by taking a nap. After the nap, she looks at the shore, still so far away. Her heart sinks. She says to herself, "It's so far! Why is it so much work? This is too hard!" She has been fighting and struggling all afternoon and still has not made progress. Enraged, she starts yelling at the shore, at the wind, at the water, at the sky that she should already be there.

In this scenario, the woman won't accept being in the middle of the lake. Raging against this fact halts progress. All that energy expended in the struggle could have been used to simply finish the journey.

I hope this sounds as ridiculous to you as it does to me. As outsiders, we can see how simple it would be to get to the other side. Yet life is exactly like this. The internal struggle is what creates so much pain when we simply need to paddle to shore. The only cost would have been some focused work and a few sore muscles.

Allowing means accepting where you are in the process of change. You can accept your opinionated self, your dysfunctional reactions, your uncomfortable feelings, all of it. You can even work with the part of you that is grieving over lost possibilities. You can stop judging the fact that you're not already perfect and healed. When you stop the struggle, you develop awareness. Awareness tells you where you are on the journey and what you can do next.

You'll likely be on the earth a bit longer, during which time you'll be stuck living with your thoughts. It is worth being kind to yourself even when you are not yet on the other side of the lake.

CHAPTER EIGHT

BASIC TROUBLESHOOTING

B elow are tips designed to reassure you and deepen your practice. Discussion about emotions being expressed refers to how they are expressed in your body. This could mean sensations such as tightness in your chest or clenching in your throat. Acting out negative emotions with external behaviors does not lead to healing.

Troubleshooting tip #1: Lean into feeling bad – even more than before.

If you recall the body focusing questions in step 2, their purpose is to get you deeply tuned in to the expression of emotion in your body. They also get you out of your story (through which your jerk brain tells you all the reasons why you should be upset).

To continue to stay focused on your body, it helps to use the modified questions below. When a negative emotion comes up, you have an opportunity to heal. Emotions do need permission to express fully. The more completely you can allow your emotion to be seen, the more quickly and thoroughly your mind can work through the healing process.

Depending on your answers to the body focusing questions from step 2, you can invite the feeling to show up completely. Here are examples of how to do so:

- If the feeling shows up as hot, I say, "Allow it to be hot. Ask if it needs to get hotter and allow that to happen." The same goes for a cold feeling: "Allow it to get as cold as it needs to get."

- If the feeling shows up as heavy, I say, "Allow it to be heavy. Ask how heavy it needs to get."

- If the feeling shows up as sharp or spiky, it can be physically painful. Even so, I say, "Let it be sharp. Ask it how sharp it needs to get. Let it be uncomfortable. This isn't forever; it's just for now. Let it be there." I add the last part to encourage them to stick with it since physical pain brings up that instinct to pull away.

- If it's tight around the lungs, throat, or heart, I say, "Let it be tight. Allow it to show you how tight it needs to get. I know it's uncomfortable. See if you can let yourself be uncomfortable."

Here you are inviting the feeling to come up all the way. Remember, part of your mind does not want to do this! That's okay. You can acknowledge that part that judges or resists, then continue to invite the feeling to come up. Whatever it felt like, ask if it needs to do that more. Tell the feeling it is allowed to do what it needs.

These examples show what it is like to allow in a radical way. We all have the impulse to suppress bad feelings. The more completely we can allow, the more healing we can accomplish.

If asking the feeling to show up all the way feels overwhelming, you can start by asking the feeling, "How much of this feeling (heat/cold/pain/tightness) is my mind ready to bring up today?" This gives your mind the allowance to address how much it can handle.

Note: These questions are for people who can handle some emotional discomfort. If you have dissociative symptoms as discussed in the warning section of chapter 5, search for a therapist that specializes in trauma. He or she will likely start by helping you learn coping skills for those symptoms and practicing the skills with you when you get emotionally overwhelmed in session. Once you're able to use those skills, you can invite the therapist to guide you through the process of therapeutic mindfulness using the handouts and practicing with them in session until you both feel you are ready to work at home.

If you do not struggle with dissociative symptoms, the above questions can move the process along more quickly.

If you find yourself wanting to do this but not trusting yourself, start with a smaller target. Perhaps feeling all the intensity of a horribly traumatic event would be too much at first. Instead, you could use a recent interaction that bothers you. Starting smaller can help you learn the process before practicing it on bigger targets.

Also, when you have a target that you're afraid to address, make the fear the target. You can ask yourself, "What if I felt all the pain of this target?" This question would make the fear very obvious. Then move to step 2 of therapeutic mindfulness while focused on the fear. Where do you feel the fear in your body? You can work on the original target another time after working through most or all the fear. Read more on this in chapter 11 on resistance.

Troubleshooting tip #2: Remember to describe the process. Make sure you're not focused on jerk brain's story (wallowing).

When the feeling in your body doesn't change, move, get better, or get worse, check whether you are thinking. This is the most common reason why the feeling is stuck. Remember, wallowing thoughts will feed the feeling because they tell you why you *should* feel bad!

If this happens to you, sometimes a simple reminder that you want to get out of your thoughts and into your body is helpful. Go through the body-focusing questions until you are tuned in to your body and out of your thoughts. For many people, once they've gone through the questions, they are completely focused on their physical experience. You might simply need to describe the feeling in more detail so you can focus on your body. Then you can go on to the allowing phrases to continue the process (step 3).

Troubleshooting tip #3: Remember that your attention must be focused. For some, this could take extra prompting.

What if your story or narrative won't stop, even when the body sensation is very clear?

For people whose thoughts take on an obsessive quality, the thoughts can intrude on the process. In this pattern, those intrusive thoughts get in the way of work, home, relationships, and most aspects of life.

If you find focus difficult and your thoughts persistent, try doing the process out loud. It's harder to get distracted by thoughts this way. When you only think, you could be giving your mind long periods of silence. Instead, use less time between asking the body focusing questions or stating the allowing phrases. You can try talking to your feeling using ideas from the "Allowing Phrases" worksheet. For example, you can remind the feeling that you're there for it and it can have all the space it needs.

Talking out loud at regular intervals will keep you on track and accountable. It's harder to daydream when you have to say something every ten seconds. It might sound something like this:

"I have a heavy ball in my chest. It feels like a fist. It is very tight, dark red, and hot. It is very uncomfortable. It feels heavy, like twenty pounds." Pause and notice.

Then: "Allow the feeling to be there. Give it all the room it needs. It just wants to be heard. I can listen and be curious." Pause and notice.

Then: "I notice the feeling is still very tight, but it is not as hot. The dark red is fading. It is still uncomfortable. Now the tightness is slightly less. It's moving down, now in my solar plexus." Pause and notice.

Then: "Allow the feeling to do what it needs. My only job is to watch. Let it do its thing."

You can also talk directly to the feeling, saying things like, "You're allowed to be here. I'll stay with you. Take all the space you need. I'll just watch."

Continuing to describe and then using ideas that focus on allowing should help you to stay out of the story and let the process move.

Another option is to record yourself making allowing statements and prompting occasionally, "What's happening in my body now?" Play the recording to keep you on track.

Troubleshooting tip #4: Remember to allow the process. Make sure you're not resisting.

Resisting takes tricky forms. Your mind is very motivated to suppress pain. Take Gwen's story:

> Gwen was new at therapeutic mindfulness and began practicing at home. A few weeks later, she had feelings of shame come up in her life, and I guided her to focus on them using therapeutic mindfulness. After a few minutes, I asked about her body sensations, and the feelings were the same. She said she was out of her thoughts and focused on her body and that she was allowing the feeling to be in her body, but she said, "My body is trying to calm down."
>
> My ears perked up immediately at the phrase "trying to calm down." Gwen believed that she was allowing and that this was her body's reaction, independent of her. I cautioned Gwen against "trying to calm down" and suggested she invite the feeling in her body to be tense, tight, and

uncomfortable while she observed. I suggested she could even be curious about what the feeling needed to do next.

After a few moments, I checked in again. This time, the feeling was quickly getting smaller and lighter. Within fifteen minutes, the feeling of shame went from the size of a golf ball to a pea and then disappeared. After the feeling cleared, a series of thoughts spontaneously popped into her mind about how to see herself with kindness.

In this example, Gwen's mind was trying to resist discomfort. Her mind tricked her into believing she was allowing and that her body was trying to calm down independently of her. And where does her body get its signals? From her, of course!

She wasn't conscious of what was happening, and that's okay. The mind is creative in its avoidance. The answer is still the same. We must remind ourselves to allow the discomfort. In this case, I helped her overcome the resistance by inviting the feeling to be more uncomfortable. This trick can break through resistance.

Immediately after Gwen invited the feeling to be there, the process moved quickly. Not only did the emotion resolve, but a new, positive way of seeing herself emerged. Her mind was able to believe kind thoughts about herself once it had worked through the story of shame.

Even after having done this process myself for a long time, when I hit a spike of emotion and go into my body, I have found that I need to tell myself deliberately, "Let the feeling be there. Open up to it." Logically I know to do this. Not only have I done it many times, but I also teach it daily! And yet, I still get that natural first reaction to resist discomfort. This gentle reminder does the trick.

You might always have the urge to lean away from discomfort. The true change is the habit of remembering more quickly, then choosing to lean into the discomfort with these gentle reminders.

Troubleshooting tip #5: Remember to allow the process. Make sure you're not judging.

Allowing means dropping the judgment. You might notice the physical sensations and tell yourself to allow them to be there, but you also have a distinct opinion about the feelings and yourself for having them! Consider what Maria experienced:

Maria thought she was allowing because she was taking the time to sit with and notice the feeling. Yet strong judgments were present. As we spoke, I learned that her inner monologue sounded something like this:

"Okay, I said I was going to sit with this feeling, and wow—it's uncomfortable! I shouldn't feel this way. It's in my chest and neck again. Why is it always in my chest and neck? You'd think I would have figured out how to stop carrying all this around! God, I'm so bad at this. Clearly, this shows I'm doing it wrong and not getting anywhere."

Remember: mindfulness is focused, *nonjudgmental* attention. Do these thoughts sound nonjudgmental to you?

Do you notice yourself spending time focused on your body, but your mind thinks you're bad for having this feeling? Do you look down on it or down on yourself for having it? What is your opinion about it?

Allowing is not a grim determination that you're going to live in a world of misery for thirty minutes which proves ultimately how weak and stupid you are! Gritting your teeth and forcing yourself through it is not a kind way to treat your wounded parts!

Allowing is a gentle process. When you allow, your thoughts soften. "It's okay for the feeling to be there." Your judgments drop and your self-talk becomes kinder. "This is just a hurt part of me. This is normal. People have hurts, and I'm working on healing."

When your thoughts are like this, you can start the simple observation that makes room for your feelings to heal.

These basic troubleshooting tips remove the primary issues I come across. If you find that you get very stuck on a particular target that seems overwhelming, or that you tend to go blank, keep reading. Chapter 9 on self-compassion and chapter 11 on resistance offer insights that could help. You could also seek wisdom from a therapist or meditation teacher.

CHAPTER NINE

HOW TO APPLY NONJUDGMENT AND SELF-COMPASSION

> The curious paradox is that when I accept my-
> self just as I am, then I can change.
> —Carl Rogers

H ave you been doing the full therapeutic mindfulness process regularly? At this point, there are no more answers for you without having experience. Try the therapeutic mindfulness process and then read on so you can learn to apply the principles in the coming chapters. As with all wisdom, intellectual knowledge only provides the motivation to act. There is no answer that can satisfy you: only an experience can satisfy. Practicing therapeutic mindfulness becomes a practice of self-compassion.

Self-compassion seems to be everywhere in the self-help world. Many people discuss the importance of self-compassion in theory, but they don't know how to apply it. It is too easy to berate ourselves when we "should" know better.

Using therapeutic mindfulness helps. It's harder to judge a random, abstract feeling in your chest the way we judge our actions. Still, you might find some judgments sneaking in. This chapter aims to shift your thinking to help you understand why you are deserving of compassion. Any idea that stands out to you and leaves you feeling gentler toward yourself is worth writing down and adding to your list of allowing phrases (see the Appendix) or affirmations (see chapter 14, "Positive Psychology").

If you sometimes get stuck and find you are judging yourself, reread this chapter. We must repeat helpful ideas until they become a habitual way of thinking.

Remember that mindfulness is *nonjudgmental, focused* attention. Judgment can slip into our minds against our best intentions. Even if we recognize *logically* that our jerk brain is telling hurtful stories, it can be hard to stop the *feeling* of how shameful or terrible we believe we (or others) are.

When bringing up a target, common judgments are as follows:

- "I should be over this by now."

- "I should just let this go."

- "I'm weak for letting this affect me."

- "I'm so stupid."

- "I'm not worth getting better."

- "This happened because I'm unlovable."

These judgments never fix anything. Shame tells us we are bad, but it cannot make us better. Shame is a jerk brain story. Jerk brain tells us that we must beat ourselves up or we won't have the motivation to change. Think about this logic: if only we are cruel enough to ourselves, we will shape up and do everything perfectly, and finally, we can be happy. To be clear, the story says that being mean to ourselves makes us happy. Does this sound right to you?

For example, imagine you have panic attacks that make you leave social functions and you worry that people will notice and think less of you. You believe you shouldn't have panic, and you feel ashamed. To solve this problem, your jerk brain gets very angry. You become hateful toward the part of you that panics and try to make it go away by hating it more.

In this scenario, you now have panic as well as self-loathing. The fear doesn't go away, however. It gets swallowed and keeps forcing its way out when it is triggered. What you push down pushes back.

Without compassion, you never have the chance to find the source of your anxiety. You're too focused on your self-hate story to notice or care that part of you is scared and needs help.

Now the fear becomes worse. *Panic disorder* is when someone who has panic attacks constantly worries about having another panic attack. They dread being exposed and judged as weak, crazy, or unacceptable. Denying the fear is like denying other emotions. They build up and get worse.

As you can see, condemning ourselves is supposed to stop the behavior, yet when the feeling is triggered, the behavior comes back even worse than before. The sad irony is that shame ensures we keep the problem. When we beat ourselves up, not only do we have the initial problem, but we have added self-judgment. Both are hurt parts of us.

We need to accept ourselves if we wish to change. This isn't some goofy platitude—it's practical. The other way simply doesn't work. But it is possible to see ourselves as humans who are both loveable and flawed humans in the process of growth.

The Purpose of the Hurt Part

Why do we carry hurt parts? Why should I have to deal with hurt at all? Why do I have old feelings with me when I know it would be better to just move on?

It's easy to judge our hurt parts when they don't make sense to our adult self. Our reactions can seem ridiculous: whether it's the widower who freezes when attempting to fold laundry (laundry being a reminder of his deceased spouse) or the young mother panicking when walking into a grocery store.

One client referred to her panic with quiet disgust, "I don't like myself very much." She saw herself as weak for having such feelings because "other people have been through worse." She could not see her own trials with compassion. In her eyes, her pain didn't count, and as a person, she didn't measure up.

Remember jerk brain's plan for happiness? If you beat yourself up enough for being stupid, you will become hypervigilant and make yourself do everything perfectly, and then you can finally be happy!

Notice: the plan is to be meaner to yourself so you can be happy.

It's not the best plan I've heard. And it doesn't work. The judgment believes you need it. What would happen if you stopped judging? If you don't judge yourself for being angry, won't that make you an explosive, hateful person? If you don't judge how weak you are, won't you be a sad-sack doormat forever? If you don't judge your mistakes, won't they happen again and again?

One more question: has judging ever worked to make you a perfect and happy person?

In contrast to the better self we had hoped for, judging ourselves makes us miserable. Because we demand perfection, we tend to get defensive when we fall short. We are fearful about our perceived defects being seen and judged by others, so we scramble, hide, defend, and counter-attack: anything to avoid these terrible feelings. Judging doesn't make us happy. Instead, it teaches us that our mistakes are shameful and that we are worthy of judgment. But because part of us believes we need the judgment, the idea of accepting our perceived faults becomes so frightening that we avoid dealing with them. This is a problem because we cannot heal what we avoid.

This is why we must accept ourselves to be able to change.

Because judging ourselves doesn't work, let's consider our hurt parts from another perspective.

Everything we do that is negative was once an adaptive mechanism. There was a time in our life when our reactions helped us survive emotionally. Many abuse survivors have feared for their lives or believed a family member was about to be killed in front of them. These responses can be a strategy for literal survival as well as emotional survival.

Let's look at examples of common survival strategies: fight, flight, freeze, and fawn.

Fight: In a scenario where a father beats a passive mother, a child might need to choose which example to identify with: the controlling father or cowering mother. By identifying with the father, this child escapes the horrible sense of vulnerability and powerlessness that comes with being a victim. The child grows into an adult so aggressive that he never has to feel weak. Unfortunately, as an adult, this person walls off real connection to others and prefers controlling them. He carries a deep fear of vulnerability and weakness throughout his life. Any situation that triggers these feelings will bring outbursts of anger and aggression.

Flight (fear): If a young child has a violent, drunken father who comes home raging, smashing things, and hurting family members, the child might have hidden to help her survive. Later in life, the adult could become hyperaware of any sign of aggression from a boss or lover. In response to irritation, she might leave physically or shut down emotionally. This reaction was created to avoid conflict, which to her is dangerous. As an adult, however, it does not help her stand up for himself.

Freeze: A common example of freeze would be a victim of sexual abuse, particularly if the abuser was threatening and the child feared for her life. The child learned to comply to survive but also created a mental link between sexual touch and extreme danger. As an adult, any unwanted sexual advance, even a hand on the knee, causes terror and a freeze reaction, creating a situation where she can easily be taken advantage of again. The freeze response overpowers her ability to function in basic ways, such as fighting back or even just making an excuse to leave the room. Brain scans and trauma research have documented such differences in the brain after trauma. You might remember the previous example of the woman who was a black belt when she was raped. She froze so completely she could not draw on her training to even attempt to fight the assault.

Fawn: If a child's mother explodes without warning, beats him, or becomes emotionally cold and does things like lock the child outdoors in wintertime, he might learn extreme people pleasing to soothe his mother's rages. In cases like this, it is a literal survival skill. The child could develop extreme sensitivity to his mother's slightest irritation, jumping in to fawn over his mother, soothing and comforting, using any known tactic to keep his mother calm. As an adult, when a significant other starts to get upset, strong anxiety rears up like a monster. The adult now caters and scrambles to make sure his lover is okay at all times so that he won't be hurt or abandoned—emotionally or physically.

In each case, these reactions helped a child get through horrible situations. In each case, the emotional brain held onto the survival tactic long after it was useful.

The purpose of trauma reactions is to survive. We might tell ourselves logically, calmly, "There's no need to react in this way. I'm grown. I'm safe now. There is no danger." But the emotional brain responds like a stubborn teenager with arms crossed, saying, "There's no way I'm giving up this reaction. We're still alive because we do things this way. What if we need it again? Nope, it's here to stay, and so am I. I'll keep us safe at all costs."

In our early years, our emotional brain believes we need acceptance to survive. Hurts that seem less dramatic can stick with us as well, creating illogical reactions. If a response makes no sense and logic cannot change it, then the response is not logical; it's emotional. Your brain is determined to survive whether it makes sense to you or not.

I've had clients describe insights about the purpose of their hurt parts. After a meditation, one client shared her insight about her jerk brain, saying, "My brain really isn't a jerk. It thinks it's trying to protect me. It's just not very good at it."

Similarly, a phobia client used therapeutic mindfulness to lean into her fear. She told me, "I realized the fear is just as afraid as I am." This breakthrough took her to a place of compassion which was calming to her fearful part.

While hurt parts don't make sense in the present, the emotional brain holds onto them until we can soothe them. Here's an example of a woman who tried as best she could to cope with a bad situation, then grew up and learned it was time to release the emotions that had once protected her:

> Cori was focusing on tightness around her jaw and neck. The feeling changed slightly but not much. I asked what would happen if she didn't have the tightness. Her mind flashed to an image of her life at age thirteen.
>
> A little history: at age thirteen Cori's mother had been gone for most of the year. Her older sister was either absent or violent. Her father was depressed. She was taking care of her younger siblings. Cori felt like she alone held everything together. She had told me of a mental picture she'd always held about that stage of her life. In it, Cori was a giant inside the house, straining against the ceiling to hold the house up with all her might, while her sister, also a giant, furiously jumped up and down on the roof.
>
> This is the time period that flashed in Cori's mind during the exercise. In her body, she still had the tight clenching around her jaw and neck. Still focused on her body, I asked what would happen if Cori did not have the tight, gripping feeling. She had the spontaneous thought: "Everything would fall apart."
>
> Cori realized that the intensity she sometimes has when dealing with all kinds of things in life comes from a thirteen-year-old who feels that she alone holds the burden and she has to fight with all her might just to keep things together.

Cori knew this intensity was not necessary in her present life. Her circumstances were not chaotic. She had much more influence in her life and she had better ways to cope. The tension and intensity she sometimes experienced (and couldn't drop easily) were outdated. She no longer needed to clench her jaw and grit her teeth and stress herself to be effective in the world. Her intensity and toughness were meant to give her the strength to keep everything together—even when nothing was falling apart!

Cori saw that she no longer needed to be strong in this way. She had strength and decided she could be calm and determined at the same time. She realized she could be even more effective when she had a clear mind not ruled by old emotions.

This session of therapeutic mindfulness showed Cori that she needed to spend more time with her hurt thirteen-year-old and nurture her. The more the thirteen-year-old becomes soothed, the more Cori's emotional brain can realize these outdated coping methods are no longer needed and the younger self can let go.

Our brain might want to help, but it reacts frantically and without wisdom. It is for us to bring wisdom into our reactions. Allowing yourself to nurture the hurt part will free you. After healing, it becomes possible to choose a new response.

Exercise 4. Identifying the Hurt Parts

If you've been stuck on an issue and you suspect you are in the habit of judging yourself, try this exercise. It begins with your standard therapeutic mindfulness procedure as described in chapter 5. (Refer to chapter 5 if you need help on how to choose and bring up a target.)

1. Bring up the target.

2. Identify what you feel and where it is in your body.

3. Identify what hurt parts of you are showing up. Common parts:

- Sad part

- Scared part

- Angry part

- Judging part

- Shameful part

- Grieving part

- Child part or younger part

- (Feel free to create a name if you don't find it on the list, such as the angsty teenager part or the self-righteous part. If the feeling is deep sadness, you could label it "the sad part of me.")

4. Which part is the strongest? Focus on that part.

5. Check for judgmental ideas. What do you think about this feeling? Are you kind to yourself about having the feeling? Or do you judge yourself? Look for these ideas:

- "I should be over this by now."

- "I'm weak/stupid."

- "I shouldn't feel this way."

- "Something is wrong with me."

- "Having this feeling means I'm a bad person."

- "Having this feeling means I'm a failure."

6. Acknowledge the judging part without getting into the thoughts, and then imagine setting it aside and refocusing on the other feeling. For example, you can tell yourself, "I see the sad part of me and see the part that is judging myself

for being sad." Then focus on the sad part in the body.

7. Now that you've identified the strongest part, you can work on healing. Use steps 2 and 3 from the therapeutic mindfulness process to describe and allow.

*Note: If you notice a shame or guilt part coming up, make this the primary focus. It is important to work through shame using the physical feeling and all tools for compassion. Shame will block other emotional work.

Practicing being the observer and identifying your parts can help train your brain to separate your identity from your jerk brain responses.

This chapter discusses how shifting from judgment to nonjudgment makes room for compassion. It is transformative to use these and any other ideas you can find to bring compassion to the parts of you that hurt. The purpose of being kind to ourselves is not to blow off responsibility—quite the opposite. When we behave badly, it is because our hurt parts are activated. They need to be healed, to be cared for. When we feel nurtured, we are no longer drawn to bad decisions. In addition, we take more responsibility because we realize that we are the ones who can and must heal ourselves.

To help accomplish this healing, let's look closer at how to accept these parts.

Accepting Our Hurt Part

Accepting our hurt parts is a powerful way to neutralize judgment.

When you have a feeling that you want to avoid, judge, or push down, think of it as a hurt part of you. We all have hurt parts. Allowing ourselves grace in our humanity is something we need to be okay.

Imagine a small child approaches you, vulnerable and crying. You ask, "What's wrong," and she says, "I'm scared." She is visibly shaking, frightened, and checking to see whether you will make room for her big emotions. Is it safe to cry? Is there comfort when she's scared?

A nurturing person would not sneer and say, "It's stupid to be afraid. You are such a weak child. Just get over it."

To nurture this child, you would get close, maybe sit on the ground or have her come and sit with you. When she's sobbing or trembling, talking doesn't get far. In this moment, you simply listen, and you might hold the child. Your full, caring attention helps the little one feel important and safe. She will eventually be comforted and become calmer. She can then share about what's going on, or perhaps this comfort was all she needed.

The process of comforting a hurt child is exactly the same process we do with ourselves in therapeutic mindfulness. When our brain holds onto unresolved hurt, part of our mind still functions at that age.

Shame for having feelings will halt the healing process. To make sense of this, think again about the trembling child. Imagine what happens when an adult shames her child instead of comforting her. Imagine the adult saying, "You're scared because of the night-mare? Well, it's stupid to cry now. Clearly, you're awake and the nightmare is over. You're such an idiot. No wonder nobody likes you."

Can you see how there will be no healing of the fear? A child would hear the message that she is bad and is not supposed to have feelings that don't make sense. She would shove down her feelings so she would not be verbally attacked by the adult and so she could be good.

The same is true each and every time we tell ourselves we're stupid for having an irrational feeling because we're grown up and should know better. Not only do we continue to carry around our hurt feelings (because we didn't heal them), but now we also carry judgment and anger at ourselves as well as a belief that feelings make us bad or weak.

There is another way. In our grief, hurt, anger, or sadness, we deeply want to be heard. In these moments, we crave connection and acceptance. Rather than judging ourselves, we can say to our own feeling, "I care about this hurt. I can give it the attention it needs. I will sit with it and allow it to show me the pain." When we allow and validate our hurts, healing can begin.

When we do this, we give ourselves subconscious messages such as the following:

- "I matter."

- "My pain matters."

- "My pain is not shameful."

- "I can accept the parts of me that are unpleasant."

- "I don't have to hide part of myself to be worthy of attention."

- "I can handle my feelings. They are not too much."

- "I am not too much."

The same principles are true regardless of which negative emotion is targeted.

When we have layers of protection keeping us from feeling, a strong emotion can bring up several parts, including a judgmental part. The story below shows a different type of therapy, but I've included it to illustrate how different hurt parts can show up.

Maggie was new to therapeutic mindfulness. When I first tried to walk her through the process, she was steeped in self-judgment.

One week, we talked about the deep sadness that arose whenever Maggie felt unheard. Exploring the sadness, Maggie shared that she felt needy for wanting her husband to listen to her deeply. Suddenly, she felt intense anger about feeling needy. She told me, "I hate that part of me. No one wants to be around a person like that."

Maggie's judgmental part believed that her neediness would define her in the eyes of other people. Another aspect of her was frightened. I suggested she focus on the needy part as only a piece of her and not all of her. This was important because her judgment about this part of herself could block her ability to heal.

I pointed out other parts of her that were practical, strong, and nurturing, all of which would not disappear if she felt needy at times. I asked her to notice all of her parts, positive or negative. She closed her eyes to imagine this. Although the needy part was very powerful, she was able to notice that she had other parts as well. I then asked her to bring up her older, wiser self to see how that version of her viewed the situation.

Maggie closed her eyes again and spent time with these ideas. Her older, wiser self yelled at the rest of her parts that the needy part was allowed to have a voice too. This was progress in trying to make room for her needy part, but Maggie was trying to force the other voices within herself to submit.

Waging battle within oneself will not lead to healing. I wanted to help her create an internal space of acceptance and nurturing instead.

I suggested she visualize all the parts in a conference room and have her older, wiser self let her other parts know that they would each get a chance to be heard. As Maggie closed her eyes and delivered this softer message, the tension in her face visibly relaxed for the first time during that session.

I had Maggie go back into her mind one more time and tell all the parts that she would come back and that they would keep working through these issues a little bit at a time. She did this successfully.

When we discussed her experience, Maggie shared that her neediness had built up over the years so much that it had felt like too much to handle. In this session, she was finally able to let her neediness have a seat at the table and recognize that this part of her felt like a little girl. She shared that although the needy part still felt strong, it no longer seemed like the only voice in the room.

Within a half hour, Maggie transformed her ability to notice her neediness calmly without fear of it owning her. Once she did this, everything softened.

This example shows how judgment can block healing and how accepting our hurt parts can neutralize judgment. When Maggie was fighting her sense of neediness, that part fought back. It screamed to be heard. Maggie then fought harder. She had years of suppressed need that fought back, and it scared her. Instead of just neediness, she ended up with neediness, fear of feeling the neediness, and deep judgment for having needs at all!

This example also illustrates the change that happens when we find a way to remove judgment and instead work on accepting the various aspects of ourselves. Once she was able to accept all of her parts, the intensity became manageable. During the exercise, she began treating herself kindly.

Maggie's story has implications for us all. Consider how she told herself that her flaws made her unworthy and that her unacceptable parts should be stomped into submission. There is neither acceptance nor compassion in this approach.

When we see our perceived flaws as parts of us that are hurting, we can notice that we have other parts capable of accepting and nurturing each other. This opens up our ability to accept kindness from ourselves and others.

The act of listening without judgment is a habit. Over time, we all can learn to be gentler to ourselves. As our hurt parts (which are always scared) become less fearful and more comforted, other areas in our lives are able to improve.

We all have layers of healing to work through.

Our Younger Part

Imagine someone toward whom you feel loving and tender. Perhaps this is a small child or a beloved pet. How would you respond if they were desperately scared or badly hurt? If you can imagine this, then you can learn how to treat your own hurt parts.

Whenever an adult's emotional reaction is more than the situation logically calls for, something from the past is feeding it. When this happens, you can focus on the emotion, then ask for a gut answer to this question, "Right now in this emotion, how old do you *feel?*" Surprising answers spontaneously pop up.

This might seem like a strange exercise, but it can be powerful. Most people can sense how young they feel in an emotion. Sadness at three feels different than sadness at thirteen. Anger at five feels different than anger at fifteen, which feels different than anger at thirty.

For those who allow themselves to go with their gut impression, there is almost always an answer to how old they feel. I then ask them to picture themselves at that age, to see through the eyes of that younger self, and imagine what they are going through. Looking at the hurt of the younger self is powerful imagery for healing.

> Karina felt strongly connected with an inner three-year-old who was filled with rage. It surprised me to see such intense anger in a child so young.
>
> At first, Karina wanted to soothe the anger, to help it go away. I coached Karina to allow her inner three-year-old to be as angry as she needed to be. At first, the child's anger escalated, challenging her adult self's acceptance. This is the same as working with actual children who believe they cannot trust you because of their experience of being rejected. Hurt children need to see that they will be accepted, even if they are angry or bad.
>
> Over time, the three-year-old's anger seemed to wear out, and Karina was still present. The three-year-old started to believe she might be acceptable. Then Karina was able to see the vast feelings beneath the anger. There was hurt and deep loneliness. This pain became the focus of Karina's work in therapy for the next three months.
>
> Being with the young feeling of hurt and loneliness taught Karina how to be kind toward herself in the face of big emotions. Her self-compassion led to healing that gave her much relief from present-day anxiety symptoms.

People tend to be furious at themselves for not reacting ideally. After clients like Karina are able to develop compassion for their younger self, they are kinder to themselves when they recognize that part showing up. When the younger self is upset and impacting the present, the person is now able to go into their body and do therapeutic mindfulness without the judgment they previously held for having irrational feelings. They learn to be gentle toward the younger self while sitting through the feelings.

This tool involves connecting to an image or impression of your younger self, then doing therapeutic mindfulness on the feelings that come up. In the same way that we allow our physical body's feelings to show up as we stay present with them, we can have an image of our hurt younger selves show up and stay present with them. Using the allowing phrases, we would encourage the younger self to share how they feel. They get to be sad, scared, or angry and not suppress the emotion.

At the same time, connecting with the younger self could bring up physical body feelings in the present. That is also fine. Either body sensations or a younger self-image can be the focus for therapeutic mindfulness.

It makes sense that our younger self needs help. When we are hurt at a young age, we don't have logic or abstract thinking to deal with it. Our logical brain isn't even developed to full adult size until we are about twenty-five years old. At three years old, the brain functions in an emotional way. If you've cared for toddlers, you know that they live completely in the emotion of the moment.

When we are emotionally wounded at a young age, the hurt keeps that same irrational and emotional quality unless we take the time to heal.

The younger self might be a teenager or a younger adult. Here's an example of a woman who learned to stop judging her parenting by looking at her younger adult self.

When asked how old she felt, Sabrina, a forty-eight-year-old woman, said she felt twenty-five. She was angry at herself for getting into a controlling and manipulative marriage in which she raised her children. She judged herself harshly for allowing them to be in that environment for so many years.

Looking at her twenty-five-year-old self, she could see more clearly the scared, determined young woman who'd thrown everything into trying to fix the relationship and create a loving family. Her younger self was dedicated to good, healthy relationships. At every obstacle, she tried to find a way to improve the marriage and the treatment of her children. She fought actively and fiercely. Sabrina simply didn't know that she could not change her husband no matter how many years of effort she tried nor how many workshops on marriage and communication skills she attended. She realized that her over-functioning was exactly what enabled her husband to under-function and remain comfortable.

Sabrina developed deep compassion for her younger self, who believed she could work hard and love her family into the life she wanted. She recognized that her twenty-five-year-old self had no understanding of the principles of manipulation and control with which her husband had been well trained while growing up. With this understanding, her self-judgment shifted. Instead of punishing herself mentally, she allowed herself kindness and grace over what she hadn't known, and she was able to give herself credit for how she handled herself as she developed an understanding of her family's dysfunction.

Hopefully, these examples illustrate how to see your parts with a compassion that we often don't allow ourselves as adults. We somehow think that now that we've grown up, it's no longer acceptable for us to feel lost, scared, alone, or angry. Don't worry: allowing those feelings to be heard doesn't mean they will take over our lives. You will still go about life in between sessions of therapeutic mindfulness, functioning as you always have. The idea is that you create time for healing. During that healing time, all feelings are allowed.

Feelings are uncomfortable, not lethal.

Whatever comes up, imagine the feeling is a hurt part and be kind to it. Let it be hurt. Feelings are uncomfortable, not lethal. If you catch yourself judging, you can notice the part of you that judges *and* the part of you that is hurt. Stay curious and observe. In this way, the part of you that observes can be like the steady, calm parent who is present for the other younger parts that come up.

Exercise 5a. The Younger Self

This exercise is designed to help you find a version of yourself that you can see with compassion. (Refer to chapter 5 if you need help on how to choose and activate a target.)

    1. Bring up the target. Make sure you sense an emotional reaction. If you don't notice any emotion, think about the target or describe it in detail until your

emotion is at a noticeable level.

2. Find that emotion in your body. Allow it to come up all the way.

3. Ask yourself: "When I feel this emotion, how old do I feel?"*Keep in mind, an emotion (fear, loneliness, anger) feels different at age five than it does at age fifteen or twenty-five. Go with whatever age pops into your head.

4. Picture yourself at that age. Notice what's going on with younger or little you. Try viewing life through his/her eyes. You can ask these questions:

   ◦ How is younger or little me doing?

   ◦ What is she or he going through?

   ◦ What does she or he need?

   ◦ Can I see him or her trying his or her best?

   ◦ Can I see him or her with kindness?

   ◦ Sit and notice seeing yourself with compassion. Continue until you are ready to finish the exercise.

Exercise 5b. Nurturing Your Younger Self

If you wish to take this exercise further, continue with the following steps:

1. Keep this child or younger part in mind. See if your mature, wiser self can approach the younger part.

2. Allow your mind to create an interaction between your mature self and your younger self.

* Remember to notice the interaction mindfully—meaning *without judgment* as you focus. It is common for the younger self to be unsure or not trust the mature self. Our hurt parts usually expect to be hurt again. Instruct your mature self to allow the younger self to have any reaction. Stay open and curious, without trying to fix the feelings of the younger self. The job of the mature self is to listen and be present.

3. Continue to have your mature self listen unconditionally to the younger self, simply being present and assuring the younger self that you will be there for her or him.

4. When you're ready to complete the exercise, assure your younger self that you will visit again to continue helping with whatever feelings are left.

5. Keep your promise. Visit again and keep working with your hurt part. It might surprise you how you can help each other.

6. For future visits, you can simply ask, "How is my ten-year-old doing?" This is enough. Your intuition will know how your younger self feels.

If this exercise was profound for you, then you have found an age that is significant for you. You can continue using this exercise with mindfulness to nurture that part of you and continue to heal. I have had many clients that regularly check with their younger selves, whether at age seven, fourteen, or twenty-two years old—whatever age that feels a hurt which still impacts them.

This method keeps them aware of their progress in healing a particular core belief or feeling.

Once a person connects with their younger selves, I find they can check anytime on how the younger part is doing. They often do this without my suggestion. Checking in seems to happen naturally.

I had a client who did a lot of therapeutic mindfulness before she moved away. She had healed some of the deep loneliness that caused her to cling to men, and she was in a new relationship. When she started dating, she felt like the man was distant but questioned whether it was just her insecurities. We had also done "parts work" in therapy and identified her fourteen-year-old self as connected with the insecurities.

After this client had moved, I received this email:

> When we last talked, I was seeing a man that I thought had walls up, and I was experiencing insecurities but had a block working through them. You helped me get past the block, and I found a safe room with fourteen-year-old me.
>
> Since then, I dated this man for a few more months, but the feeling of him holding me at arm's length never left. I trusted that and called him out. This led to the end of us, which hurt but felt right. I wanted this relationship with all of my being because it was so fun and fit into my life here perfectly. The only thing wrong was this feeling. You helped teach me how to trust myself, and while it was hard to walk away from something amazing, it felt like the right thing to do.
>
> He has since told me that he cheated on me while I was traveling, and I couldn't help but be surprised at how right my gut was. If I hadn't trusted my gut, this could have gone on for months or years, and the hurt would have been so much more. I am grateful for the work you've led me through and the tools you've taught me so that I could walk away.
>
> Yesterday as I was practicing, I found myself in the room (now known as my safe room) with fourteen-year-old me and having the discussion that even though we were scared and not wanted by him that we were still real and loveable. And the physical pain in my chest grew and burned, and then she (fourteen-year-old me) touched it, and it filled me with love and strength. I tell you this all because it has been a life-changing gift: the ability to deal with hard things, be kind while doing so, and to move through them.

The healing power of our subconscious mind is awe inspiring. When we nurture our younger selves, they can nurture us in return. Although we did not have the resources to address and heal things that happened at a younger age, we can go back and create the healing that we have always needed.

When we force feelings away so we can function, that hurt part stays with us and waits. It shows up when we feel that way again. Being with the younger part helps us move past judgment and finally learn to be kind to all aspects of ourselves.

When you spend time with a younger or child version of you, in your head the child can have reactions that you weren't expecting. They might be angry or closed off. Accept this younger version. Stay with him or her. Allow him or her all the feelings he or she didn't get to show the first time around.

This is a great time to practice allowing. Your mind is expressing a part of you that needs to show up this way. Allowing the child part to be how they need to be while showing that you won't judge them or leave them is very powerful. Nonjudgment builds trust that you won't reject yourself, and the hurt child part can start to heal.

Using this process, we get to experience true acceptance.

The Role of Self-Compassion in Healing

Is self-compassion worth all the hype? Is it worth all this work?

I say absolutely – I have zero doubt. In my work as a therapist, I've helped some people experience profound healing. And yet some people don't seem to heal at all, even after a year or more of therapy. As I observed the differences between those individuals, I came to believe the reason is a lack of self-compassion.

Therapists are supposed to be able to see their clients with *unconditional positive regard*—a concept introduced by Carl Rogers in the 1950s and used universally in therapy since. Clients should be able to share their darkest thoughts and feelings and still be received with compassion. A therapist should be able to see clients' strengths and humanity, even when clients cannot.

Mind you, this is not how a therapist should *act*. It is how a therapist should actually view the client. A therapist's perception impacts therapy in many ways.

Some people are genuinely helped by this aspect of therapy. For others, it does not seem to matter. The therapist can share the good they see in a client. If a client mentally rejects the compassionate views of the therapist, it will not help. The client won't believe that any positive feedback has to do with them. If the client perceives the therapist as genuine, then the therapist is either seen as nice or simply naïve because their good opinion cannot possibly reflect the client's worth.

Humans can only accept compassion, kindness, or empathy from others to the extent that we are able to internalize it—to believe it ourselves.

Think about someone you know who can't accept compliments. You and others genuinely have liked and complimented this person for years, but she still criticizes herself harshly. Even if she believes you mean it, she doesn't believe it is true. This is why we need to love ourselves before we can accept love.

If you hear how this type of person speaks to herself, you can see the self-judgment. Mindfulness cannot coexist with judgment. Compassion cannot coexist with judgment. To heal, we must move from judgment to compassion.

The first thing we need is to develop the habit of catching when we are judging ourselves for our feelings or reactions. If you are human, the judgment will happen. We need a better way to respond.

Many of the exercises in this book have the purpose of enhancing your mindfulness skills. If you find self-judgment, shame, or guilt coming up, it is imperative that you use any and all means, including those discussed herein, to look past those judgments. It's as I say to my clients:

Judgment blocks healing.

I cannot emphasize this enough. **Judgment blocks healing.** If you are bewildered by certain people who seem to struggle and never heal, this one idea likely holds the answer.

We need to find a way to catch and shift our tendency to judge ourselves harshly. Naturally, there are several approaches we could take, and chapter 14, "Positive Psychology," has a few exercises to help you learn ways to view and speak to yourself kindly. First, it is important to both acknowledge the part of you that judges yourself and to find a shift in perspective as a foundation for your work.

Switching to a Compassion Mindset

Our feelings are valid. We need to learn that it's okay to feel bad even when it doesn't fit our logic.

We must practice validating our pain if we are to learn self-compassion. Validating our pain is the first step toward healing. It does not mean we validate bad behaviors or our jerk brain's stories.

Below is a common example that shows feelings that are valid when the story is not.

Arthur was raising his five-year-old daughter, Taylor, who sometimes spent weekends with her mother. One night, a fly found its way into Taylor's room. Arthur checked in on Taylor long after she had been put to bed. Taylor was staring wide-eyed, jumping and jerking her head each time the fly moved. She did not like flies, but on this night she had worked herself up into a state of intense fear.

Taylor had been around flies before. Clearly, no fly had killed nor maimed her. There was no traumatic fly experience. Still, Taylor was in a state of near terror.

Taylor's human experience of feeling intense fear is very simply human even though her story about why she was so scared was foolish. When the level of emotions doesn't match the circumstance, that's a clue:

It's not about the fly.

Luckily, Arthur is a very intuitive and caring father. He took Taylor to another room and stayed with her until she calmed somewhat. After a while, Arthur was able to ask Taylor some gently probing questions, only to find out that conflict had escalated at her mother's house. Taylor was afraid of the anger and fighting within that household.

Over time, this pattern would continue. The "fly phobia" would intensify when there was conflict or when her mother didn't see her for several weeks due to traveling. At ages five and six, a child doesn't say, "Daddy, I'm worried about Mommy," nor is she aware of the problem. A child reacts to something in the environment with the fear she is carrying inside.

Arthur had the insight to respond to his daughter's fear rather than getting angry that Taylor was behaving irrationally over a fly. By listening to her feelings, Taylor calmed, and then she was able to talk more about scary things in her life.

Her fear was valid—not in the current situation, but in the context of a human struggling with emotion. And her fear is much more relatable when we know its source.

All emotions are more relatable when we uncover the origins. Often, we can't do this until *after* we work through the emotion.

Your emotions are valid. All of them. Even if you're scared for a reason that feels "stupid," fear is fear. It feels terrible. Even if you are depressed and you can't understand why it is still painful. Even if you are angry when you "should not be," the anger still hurts you and others. Your human experience of emotions is valid because your humanity is worthy of compassion.

Your human experience of emotions is valid because your humanity is worthy of compassion.

Although emotions are valid, your logic or actions might not be valid. When you are angry, running someone over with a car is not a good move for you or them! When emotional, thoughts are often faulty (i.e., "They've ruined my life"), but the internal experience of anger is something we can care about and work to heal.

Our feelings *are* valid, and it is *still* our responsibility to heal them.

To say a feeling is valid means that it is worthy of empathy and compassion. This is true for adult life, not just childhood fears. We can change our habits by catching the tendency to dismiss our feelings, such as when a person complains bitterly, then suddenly says, "But it's okay. I'm over it." When we catch ourselves, we can then admit how we're feeling. This is the time to use therapeutic mindfulness.

When we heal, we sometimes realize an extremely stressful issue now feels perfectly fine. I see this often when people do therapeutic mindfulness. Just like with the story of the fly phobia, adults have fears (and other emotions) that logic does not cure.

Overall, remember to be gentle with yourself. We all face a fly at times in our lives, and it's never about the fly. A great deal of work in therapy is done by going beneath the story to explore the feelings or core belief that is at the root of the pain.

Once we stop second-guessing ourselves and start acknowledging our feelings, we have the option to meet them with empathy. It is more powerful than words can convey to share your deep thoughts and secrets and then have them met with empathy—especially your own.

We must work to overcome judgment and shame and practice nurturing ourselves. We need not heal alone, but ultimately, we do heal ourselves.

Exercise 6: Practicing Gentleness

The purpose of this exercise is to train our brain to react to hurt parts with gentleness. It will focus on this idea: I am learning to be gentle with myself as I heal.

Your work from exercise 4 will help as we begin by identifying hurt parts.

1. Think about a situation or person that always gets you stuck emotionally.

2. Notice the different points of view or parts in your head. For example:

   ○ Part of me feels irritated at it/them.

   ○ Part of me feels, if I am really honest, hurt by it/them.

   ○ Part of me feels scared to look at how deep the hurt is.

   ○ Part of me feels little, like being a kid all over again.

   ○ Part of me feels angry at myself for being affected by it/them at all.

   ○ Part of me is grieving for what I hoped would be.

   ○ Part of me judges myself. (Why can't I just get over it?)

   ○ Part of me is just plain tired.

- ◦ Part of me thinks this exercise isn't working.

3. Name or describe the parts to make them clear. Looking above, we can see the following:

   - ◦ An angry part

   - ◦ A hurt part

   - ◦ A young or childlike part

   - ◦ A grieving part

   - ◦ A judging part

   - ◦ A tired part or avoidant part

   - ◦ A pressuring, distracting, or critical part

4. Keep naming reactions and feelings as a part of you until you can find no new parts. Write them down. When you are done naming parts, ideally you will be viewing through the eyes of the last part—the one that observes the other parts. This observer part does not have an opinion about what it sees except perhaps curiosity and openness. If you have a negative view, that is another hurt part. We always want to get to the observer part.

5. For the first hurt part, say the following: "My _____ part exists to help me. I am learning to be gentle with myself as I heal this part. I care about this part of me."

6. Pause and notice the feeling of being gentle toward the part. Notice how the part reacts.

7. Repeat steps 5 and 6 for each part.

8. End the exercise by reflecting again on the main idea: "I am learning to be gentle with myself as I heal."

(Note: If you felt resistance to steps 5 and 6, i.e., "I can't be gentle with my angry part!" this indicates another hurt part.)

After you are finished, write down the areas of resistance that came up. Remember that there is no wrong outcome. What you experience is information to guide your next steps. Places where you felt resistance could be targets for future sessions of therapeutic mindfulness. You could also discuss them with a therapist or a supportive person in your life. Some people find it helpful to journal after these exercises.

This chapter discussed the importance of self-compassion and explored various mind-sets that help develop self-compassion. If you want more tips on how to give yourself the unconditional positive regard that we so desperately need for growth, you might find it useful to read books by Buddhist monks. A large part of their practice is active development of compassion for self and others. If you have other sources of wisdom on compassion, such as wise authors or religious texts, it could be useful to revisit those sources while reflecting on how you treat your hurt parts.

CHAPTER TEN

GOING DEEPER – CORE BELIEFS

I f you are thinking or feeling something, you are not alone. You did not invent a new bad thought. You did not create a new bad feeling. For example, you are not the first person to believe the following:

- If that person in my life would just do things differently, I could be happy.

- If I do enough for them, I will finally feel worthy of love and approval.

- I am a fraud and if only they (coworkers, friends, anyone) knew the real me, they would reject me.

- I am broken, worthless, or trapped or need to be in control.

- If I let my feelings out, I will literally go crazy.

These are common beliefs with which people struggle. Such thoughts reflect subconscious core beliefs that rule our emotional reactions. This chapter will explore core beliefs and their impact on our lives.

What are core beliefs and why are they important?

You might remember from chapter 3 that it is not useful to be wallow. Repeating jerk brain's story gets us more and more upset.

Sometimes we explore thoughts because we think we can find a solution. Merely analyzing an emotional problem doesn't help because the surface situation is not what bothers us. It is what we believe deep down that shapes our experience.

It is always about our core beliefs, the underlying, usually subconscious beliefs we hold about ourselves and the world. When the messages are negative, we suffer.

For example, if a person is turned down for a job and her core belief is, "I am not good enough," she could go into a spiral of self-loathing and depression. She might tell herself the rejection proves she is a failure and review all the reasons she is inadequate. She then spins a story about her endless list of perceived defects. The more energy she spends in this story, the more proof she finds and the worse she feels.

If, however, a person who is turned down for a job has the core belief, "I am capable," she will not go into a depressive spiral. She might be disappointed, but she will assume that someone very capable got the job and that another good opportunity awaits her.

You can find core belief worksheets by googling "EMDR core belief clusters PDF." Here are a few negative core beliefs that I see very commonly in therapy:

- I'm not safe.

- I'm not good enough.

- There's something wrong with me.

- I'm unstable.

- I'm alone.

- I'll be rejected.

- I need to be in control.

Beliefs about others or the world also tie into core beliefs about ourselves:

- You aren't capable. (I am alone in this/I am responsible.)

- You need to be saved. (I need to be in control/I am responsible.)

- The world is cruel. (I am in danger/I will be rejected, abandoned/I am unloved.)

If you have ever wondered why some therapists have shocking insight into your problems, it is because they listen for these fundamental beliefs underneath your stories. Consider this example:

> David had been practicing therapeutic mindfulness but found himself in a downward depression cycle. He shared concerns about literally every major area in his life. After some discussion, I learned that David had quarreled with his partner just before the depressive spiral, after which everything in his life seemed overwhelming.
>
> Most of his life had not changed a bit from the last session. It became clear that once his core belief, "I'm inadequate," was triggered, he had wallowed for the last week and spiraled until he "had a breakdown," in his words. His despair was so great that his friends were concerned about his safety.
>
> As with many a client, David felt pride in being able to "figure things out" with his intellect. He thought this was sure to help. Yet his analyzing was feeding his pain. As he shared each scenario, I heard the core belief, "I'm inadequate."
>
> "I had to leave work because I couldn't keep it together." *I'm inadequate.* "My romantic partner will leave me. I always screw things up." *I'm inadequate.* "I've become a burden to my friends. I don't know why they even bother trying to help me." *I'm inadequate.* "I can't even turn to my family because I haven't made steps to improve those relationships." *I'm inadequate.*
>
> Can you hear other core beliefs?
>
> I suggested a few closely related core beliefs that fit his statements. David resonated most with the statement, "I'm inadequate." While this core belief was triggered by the fight with his partner, it bled into everything. To fix every perceived defect he could think of felt impossibly overwhelming.

Working through how one fight activated one belief was uncomfortable, but possible.

David's story highlights the difference between analyzing and finding a core belief. Before our talk, David's analysis sent him down an endless rabbit hole where he found more and more so-called "evidence" of being inadequate. Each new train of thought made him feel worse. By the time he was done, he thought his whole life was a failure, and his depression was becoming dangerous. After our talk, David realized the problem was a specific belief rather than every aspect of himself and his life. This gave him hope and a focus to work on. This is the power of core beliefs.

How to Use Core Beliefs

If you learn to identify your core beliefs, you can cut through the jerk brain narrative and work on the actual problem. When you have a target memory or image, identifying the core beliefs brings you to the heart of why that target is emotionally painful. When you heal the core belief, the pain disappears, and there will be nothing left to trigger.

Using of core beliefs greatly enhances emotional work, including therapeutic mindfulness.

Start with step 1 of the procedure, Choosing a Target (see chapter 5, "How to Practice Therapeutic Mindfulness"). Find a target, just as you've been doing in your regular practice. (You have been practicing by now, yes?) Once you have it, read through the Core Belief Worksheet you found online to help you identify one or two primary core beliefs that feel most connected to the target. By simply reading through the worksheet, you will likely feel the relevant core beliefs jump out at you.

As you activate the target by describing an upsetting memory or situation, notice how it connects to that core belief. For example, one woman remembered terrifying memories as a young girl wherein her mother confided wanting to kill herself. At the time, she believed, "I am responsible for keeping my mother alive and I need to be in control."

If you choose to work with these using therapeutic mindfulness, you simply add the core belief when describing the target. After you bring up the target and find the core belief, continue the process of therapeutic mindfulness as normal, which means doing steps 2 and 3, describe and allow.

The core belief will help clarify what you are working on. Once you identify the strongest one, you will see jerk brain's favorite negative beliefs popping up again and again. One person will come back again and again to "I am abandoned," or "I am alone." Another will almost always go to, "I'm not good enough." Do not be discouraged when you find the same core belief popping up again. This is useful information about what's underneath all the noise in your head and where you can make substantial progress in healing.

Knowing your key core beliefs can give you a focal point. Whenever you explore a target and relate it to a core belief, you have an opportunity to chip away at something that is at the center of your emotional reactions. Deep beliefs will pop up all over the place at first. You will be able to watch yourself change as you continue to work on that belief when it comes up in different memories or scenarios. As you do the work, you loosen its hold on you.

Exercise 7: Practice Finding Core Beliefs Using Common Fictional Characters

As a break from our usual form, here is a creative exercise. I'll bring up several popular fiction characters from fantasy, comic books, and science fiction. Use the Core Belief Worksheet and guess from which core beliefs the characters are reacting. You can look up famous characters online or use those below.

If you've decided to use this as a party game (clearly a natural by-product of this book), feel free to discuss different answers with friends.

Scenario 1. *Game of Thrones*: Daenerys. As Daenerys Targaryen becomes more severe, she burns the Tully father and son for not "bending the knee." She did not listen to Tyrion Lannister's counsel on mercy. What is her core belief?

WARNING: SPOILERS BELOW!

Possible answer: "I need to be in control." "I am in danger." "I am alone." It would appear that as Daenerys's story evolves, she becomes more intense when she does not feel people are loyal. In her past, this has led to her life being threatened many times. Disloyalty means not just being out of control but being in mortal danger.

Scenario 2. *Harry Potter*: Snape. Based on his association with the Dark Lord, Snape didn't appear to be overly compassionate or have a need to be on high moral ground. And yet as you reach the end of the series, Snape shares his memories showing that he has always acted with Dumbledor and the "good guys" from the beginning of the series because of his devotion to Harry's mother who was kind to him. When he displays his animosity toward most people, in particular Harry, what might his core beliefs be?

Possible answer: "I can't trust." "I'll be rejected." "I'm alone." Looking into his memories as a youth, it is clear how other teenagers rejected Snape and ridiculed him for being different. We know Harry reminds him of Harry's father, whom Snape sees as arrogant and with whom he has painful memories. At the same time, Snape is not especially friendly. That distance appears to keep him intimidating and safe from being rejected again.

Scenario 3. *Batman.* Batman's life is spent chasing criminals as a vigilante. In general, what core beliefs drive him to this?

Possible answer: "I am not safe." "The world is not safe." This seems the most obvious and true, as his family was a target and his parents were murdered.

Scenario 4. *Batman.* Batman is close with Alfred but keeps new relationships and women at bay. In some comics and shows, Catwoman is a romantic interest that he is drawn to but sometimes pushes away. What core beliefs might be in play here?

Possible answer: "I'm abandoned. People leave me." "I am alone." The sense of abandonment can be due to his parents' death or fear that people will leave by choice.

Another angle: "I need to be in control," and "I'm responsible." When people suffer tragedy at a young age, often the way they try to avoid that pain is to control everything. Taking on the responsibility of all possible dangers and trying to control all factors might be part of Batman's belief system.

Scenario 5. *Star Trek* original series: Dr. McCoy. Dr. McCoy seems to be the lovable grouch, always grousing about how things are done and about the burdens placed upon him. And yet he is always there to go above and beyond, as long as you can handle his griping. What might his core beliefs be?

Possible answer: "I am responsible." "I need to be in control." Dr. McCoy's insistence on criticism reminds me of people that try to make things perfect out of fear. Dr. McCoy seems to try to control the circumstances by trying to get people to do what he thinks is right.

What other characters can you use to explore core beliefs? Try perhaps: Sherlock Holmes, Black Panther, Killmonger (for contrast), Captain Marvel, Wonder Woman, Katniss Everdeen, etc.

This game helps to explore how core beliefs create people's reactions. Hopefully, that is accompanied by a sense of compassion and taking others' reactions less personally. When you practice on yourself, always make room for compassion. Everyone has a healing path. The exercise should help you realize that you don't have to fix all the little problems you perceive. You primarily need to work on healing the beliefs that interrupt you from being your relaxed, loving self.

Core Beliefs and Anxiety

Core beliefs around anxiety are closely tied to our resistance to feeling pain. If you've always been "an anxious person," practicing therapeutic mindfulness can be your ticket to reducing or eliminating your anxiety.

When we avoid something we find uncomfortable, we give ourselves the subconscious message: "That would have been horrible. That's why I needed to avoid it." We end up believing our jerk brain's story about how bad that something would have been. We might even believe things like, "I can't handle hard things."

Whether we were just uncomfortable or truly frightened, the intensity with which we run from a situation feeds our subconscious belief of how scary it must be. The running itself creates more anxiety. It is a self-fulfilling prophecy.

In contrast, when we face something uncomfortable or fearful and make it through to the other side, as we do in this process of therapeutic mindfulness, we give ourselves new messages such as the following:

- "I was able to face my fear and be okay."

- "I am stronger than I thought."

- "I can do hard things."

- "My feelings are not too much for me."

- "I am not too much."

It often surprises people the first time they ride the wave of emotion and find calmness on the other side. It amazes them that they can be fine after facing hard things. Therapeutic mindfulness builds confidence and strength. The first time is often a revelation. The second time is a confirmation. As people practice therapeutic mindfulness more and more, they learn that they have the ability to face and feel hard feelings successfully. The need to run goes away. The anxiety goes away.

The core belief of anxiety is perpetuated by avoidance. It is dispelled with the practice of therapeutic mindfulness.

CHAPTER ELEVEN

RESISTANCE

The word *resistance* is sometimes seen negatively in mental health, and this tendency has not benefited us. Resistance is our mind's attempt to protect us. We all want to avoid intense negative feelings. Why wouldn't we? Often, resistance is subconscious and not under our control.

I've known people eager to dive head-first into difficult things, only to find fear and pain that stop them in their tracks. Consciously, they want to get through it, and sometimes they try to force themselves to do more, to push harder. Unconsciously the fear and pain cause them to freeze, dissociate, or panic. Remember how emotions are stronger than logic? Being cooperative does not mean we can override a subconscious need to protect ourselves.

This chapter discusses typical ways resistance can subconsciously attempt to block the process of healing. It also explores ways to work through these issues while being gentle with ourselves.

I've come to believe that forcing ourselves through very difficult emotions in spite of terror is not kind, nor is it effective. Trauma therapists know that pushing too hard when the mind is not ready traumatizes a person again. Instead, we can work through the fear and pain as they show up, healing the layers of protection and building trust that the process helps us feel better.

We need to learn *through experience* that we can do hard things.

The ability to face discomfort improves every time we successfully do therapeutic mindfulness because this practice teaches us that we can make it through to the other side of pain and that we gain so much when we do. With repeated practice, we learn that we are stronger than our feelings. The more we experience this, the less power pain and fear will have over us.

When your mind has pockets of discomfort that are especially fear-filled, resistance can rear its head in new and creative ways. While working through resistance, self-compassion is more important than ever. Be careful not to beat yourself up when your mind resists. Because it *will*. The trick is to catch it and then remember to be kind.

Spiritual Bypassing

Spiritual bypassing refers to using spiritual practices to avoid emotional pain. This is a special way the mind tricks us because it seems on the surface that we're doing the right things.

For example, meditating on peace and happiness seems like a good way to become a loving person and get over our hurts. While such meditations can be a deeply enriching practice, we must be cautious about denial. Growth does not come from ignoring the negative aspects of our experience. My friend, Emma, shared her personal experience of spiritual bypassing.

> Emma and I met for coffee after she read my blog article on therapeutic mindfulness. She shared her story of emotional healing after her divorce. Living in California at the time, she had delved into a steady meditation practice. Peers in her spiritual circle were commenting about how well she was progressing. They encouraged Emma to take her practice to the next level; to start studying at the ashram.
>
> For some reason, Emma intuitively decided to back away from this path. She told me, "Looking back, I realize I had been spiritually bypassing for almost two years. Once I stopped meditating and felt the pain around my divorce, I got over it pretty quickly."

Because Emma avoided her negative feelings, they waited for her, as they always do. Meditating to feel calm in the moment did not remove the deep need to acknowledge her pain in an accepting way.

She called it spiritually bypassing because some people in spiritual circles try to skip (bypass) the part of life where we are human and messy. They want to jump to the part where they are enlightened or blissed out. So would I if it were possible! While I love that such people want to be peaceful and loving—something to which we all should aspire—we can actually stunt our progress when we refuse to acknowledge the parts of us that feel angry, jealous, petty, hurt, or afraid.

Here's a common exchange I've had with clients:

Client: (After telling me some story of mistreatment or betrayal.) "...and that's typical of my mother." (Sighs, switches tone.) "But she did the best she could. It's okay."

Me: (In skeptical tones.) "Is it? Is it really?"

Client: "Well, no, but I know she was trying. She had a hard time growing up."

Me: "But is it really okay? When you told me that story, it looked like you were really hurt."

Client: (Concedes.) "That's true. I tend to do that a lot—just say it's okay and shrug it off."

Me: "I love that you want to not judge her and to think kind thoughts. But we can be badly hurt by people who tried their best. You can have compassion for her and still have compassion for how you were hurt by her limitations."

This conversation happens when I can clearly see emotional reactions as someone tells me a tale of woe and then I see them quickly blow off their feelings because they want to be "a good person."

Having compassion and understanding for others is a wonderful trait to develop. However, having compassion and understanding for ourselves is also needed—more, in fact. Unless we learn to validate our own feelings, we will believe the core belief that negative feelings make us bad. We will teach others, including our children, that they should swallow their negative feelings. If we all follow these teachings, everyone is blocked from the very emotional wounds that they need to heal. Wounded people are less able to be the loving selves they so deeply wish to be.

We cannot skip over our hurts when they need to be heard. If we try to bypass our pain in order to be the loving people we idealize, the buried pain will show up as helplessness or resentment. Learning to be loving toward our own hurts is a way to both validate our feelings and bring compassion to others. First, we work on our own pain. As we heal, our resentment toward the other will start to heal also. In addition, we teach those around us what it looks like when a person is allowed to feel.

Shortly after learning the term *spiritual bypassing*, I attended a spiritual conference in Boston. A friend arranged my accommodations with some of the conference organizers in a very large home. Also staying were some of the speakers, other organizers, and several conference regulars. I was staying with the "in crowd," and yet I noticed the conversation was oddly formulaic. No one shared anything personal. They did not laugh at very plain jokes. The only comments that were received well conformed to the jargon of the spiritual texts that we read.

The fear of conflict and the desire to belong and "be spiritual" seemed to have replaced authenticity. These leaders were trying so hard to seem enlightened, and yet they were missing opportunities to connect with others and to use the wisdom of the spiritual text to address their very human lives. Instead, they displayed fake serenity. Sometimes I would get a glimpse through the cracks of a person's façade, but only briefly.

I found the spiritual material to be transformational. I think this is true for all major religions and spiritual texts. Practicing peaceful states can also have life-changing effects. However, we cannot bypass our hurt parts and simply will ourselves to be in an enlightened state. We must be able to look at all aspects of our experience, both negative and positive. If we cannot look at the negative, we reinforce fear.

It's after we go through the storm that we realize the power of our resilience.

Toxic Positivity – A Synonym

Just as some people in spiritual communities want to jump past discomfort and feel blissed out, those in the self-help community or in therapy sometimes want to jump to forgiveness and love. To forgive and love is a wonderful goal. However, if we try to force it and act as if we are in a state of perpetual love while ignoring resentment and hurt, these feelings build up. Resentment and hurt don't go away just because we want them to.

We must learn to acknowledge and work on our dark side. I had this very conversation with a client who did not realize his mind was using self-help ideas to find new ways around doing the work on his feelings:

> James came across the idea of *loving your path*. He felt drawn to this,
> thinking it might be the answer. For him, loving your path meant loving
> his anger, pain, and trials.

However, James's description might not have been what loving your path was supposed to mean. Since I was well aware of James's struggle with avoidance, his description didn't sit quite right with me. I wondered if it was another form of toxic positivity—meaning false positivity that becomes a way to avoid facing our emotional work.

Let's say we are trying to love our pain. What happens when we have something in our path that is too painful for us to love? What if there is the death of a beloved spouse, parent, or child? I can't imagine a person loving the pain while grieving such a loss. If we try to love our path, not only will we still have the pain and grief, but we'll also have guilt and frustration toward ourselves because we are not loving the pain and grief. I imagine jerk brain creating a monologue like this:

"Yes, my best friend and companion is gone, but we had forty-five years together. I should be grateful. I've been given so much in life. I'm very lucky. Why can't I just let it go? So much for loving my pain! If I were doing this right, I would be glad for what I've had. It just shows how weak and damaged I am. I'm a failure even when trying to be good."

I've known people who avoided their grief for decades. When it showed up years later, they were angry at themselves for not being over it. But how could they be over it when they never faced their grief?

Loving your path sounds nice—except when you *don't* love it. If we hate something we are going through, we need to acknowledge the hate before we can heal. We cannot heal what we hide. If we try to force ourselves to love it, we give ourselves the subconscious message that part of us is unacceptable and needs to be buried. The irony here is that it's only when we accept the hate, resistance, grief, sadness, or fear that it's possible to heal them.

We cannot heal what we hide.

Remember, all feelings are valid. After they are healed, we might then come to *love the growth* that we've had and learn to feel gratitude for our path.

This is worth emphasizing: Loving your path comes *after* healing, not before. This is one of the reasons why positive affirmations by themselves are often useless. A practice like therapeutic mindfulness, where you deal with the hurt, is often the missing piece needed for growth.

> I shared my thoughts with James and asserted that a more realistic goal would be to work on accepting his path, particularly when he hates it. Accepting that we have to deal with something uncomfortable allows us to face it and work on it. In this case, accepting is not resignation. It means acknowledging what we are dealing with, then doing the work to heal.
>
> James came to understand this on a deep level within the same session. As I guided him in therapeutic mindfulness, James got in touch with intense feelings. His face contorted with rage and pain. He felt intensely angry that he should have had to deal with any of this in the first place. He raged against his treatment by others and the scars he still carried. I helped him lean into it using ideas from the "Allowing Phrases" handout and ideas from chapter 9 on compassion.
>
> It was overwhelming, but after a while, the clouds began to clear. James came to understand that it was ridiculous to think he was ever going to love that type of anger and hurt while he was carrying it. However, by accepting and leaning into it, he was able to release some of it and feel authentically better. James acknowledged that he likely had jumped at the philosophy of loving your path from his long-held tendency to avoid the shadows in his mind.

The philosophy of love your path packaged the avoidance in a way that seemed positive to James. His subconscious mind wanted to skip the pain and jump right to the feel-good stuff. After working with the anger he still carried, he could see the release of intensity, and he knew his work was not finished.

Only by addressing the positive *and* negative do we grow and heal.

A core theme of this book is that the mind comes up with all kinds of advice and justification to avoid getting uncomfortable. By reading the various forms of avoidance, hopefully, you can catch when your patterns pop up and get back on track with your healing work.

How to Roll with Resistance

What do you do when a feeling is stuck and nothing in this book so far has worked? Let's explore.

Therapeutic mindfulness is a skill. You wouldn't teach stunt driving to a teenager in their first week of driving. Similarly, the advanced techniques illustrated here will not likely help until the basic skills have been acquired. As with many skills, even advanced practitioners stay sharp by reviewing the basics so their foundation remains solid. For this reason, it might be a good idea to return to this chapter after you have been practicing the therapeutic mindfulness process from chapter 5 and reviewed chapters 8 and 9 on troubleshooting and compassion to resolve problems that have come up.

If you have been practicing and are still getting stuck, there are a few more things to try. In general, a persistent sense of being stuck is often related to very deep-seated, stuffed emotions or blocking judgments. I would recommend working with a therapist at this point. Even if you're doing great work at home, it might help to have the extra support and to practice experiencing emotions with another human being who can validate those emotions. A therapist can give an outside perspective and insight as you unravel your story. Also, some people must slowly lower their defenses and practice being vulnerable in a safe space. It is up to you to seek the support necessary for your mental health and to listen to your inner voice about when this is appropriate. For working on trauma, it is generally a good idea to have extra help.

Feeling blocked is common when people carry a great deal of guilt, shame, or fear. Overwhelming fear is often the fear of experiencing deep hurt. This happens when the feeling is so big that it seems like it will break the person. When someone has anger that overpowers other feelings, it is likely that vulnerable feelings lie beneath the anger.

It's common to be unaware as to why you feel blocked. That's the point of the block—to hide the things your mind thinks you cannot handle. Mental blocks feel much more comfortable than guilt, shame, fear, or pain. They are the mind's tools of emotional survival—which is why you should have compassion for yourself when you get stuck.

Here are a few examples of how resistance shows up as well as strategies to try.

What Does a Block Feel or Look Like?

Often clients will simply say the feeling seems stuck and it doesn't move. Remember to give the feeling a little time to be as it is and to use allowing phrases before deciding it is stuck. If it stays stuck for several minutes, check the troubleshooting steps in chapter 8. Sometimes the feeling doesn't want to move, even after giving it some space to be stuck.

Sometimes a client receives an image or impression of a physical thing blocking the feeling. One client got an image of a dam holding back all of his strong emotions. Only a trickle was available. Were the dam to be breached, the flood of emotions would be too much. That thought brought up fear.

Another client sensed a shield holding her emotions in. She could imagine peeking carefully over the top of the shield, but it felt big and impenetrable. She felt a strong need to stay behind the shield.

These and similar images, such as a wall or a cage, are fairly common. People cannot work on emotions unless they feel safe. Fear of overwhelming emotion does not feel safe. They might need to practice, perhaps on less intense targets, until they develop confidence that they can experience emotions without breaking.

If you are going through this, check with your inner wisdom, not your impulsive side. Do you need to start smaller? Or does it feel right to take a look past the block at this time? If it does, here are some strategies:

1. Ask the mind how much it is ready to handle.

Lisa had long held a great deal of fear about leaning into her emotions. She was known to space out when things got intense.

In one session she became emotional, and I asked if we could dive into the feeling. She agreed but was apprehensive, sensing she couldn't let all the emotion come up because it would overwhelm her. I suggested she ask her mind to bring up however much emotion it was ready to look at today.

She tried this and was amazed. Instead of trying to push herself into bringing it all up, she allowed her mind discretion to bring up as much as it was ready for. In turn, the battle in her mind relaxed because she wasn't trying to force anything. By accepting instead of struggling against herself, her mind allowed more emotion than was typical for her.

While it is transformative to allow the feeling to come all the way up, everyone is different. If that is too frightening, this is one tool to try. Lisa would try to push herself prematurely while fighting against herself. Trying to force the mind is neither kind nor compassionate. By accepting where her mind was and allowing the experience to unfold, her mind relaxed.

If you feel blocked, invite the feeling to come all the way up. Most people I see are able to do this. Keep in mind, these people are also able to function in daily life and tolerate some emotion.

If you invite the feeling to surface and notice a strong reaction, like your mind screaming, "I can't handle that!" remember to be gentle with yourself. You never want to force your mind; instead, roll with the resistance. You can say to yourself, "Okay, I'm not ready for all of it. How much can I do today?" Then allow yourself to work with that much. It really is okay to do this. No one heals everything in one go, so in truth, everyone is working on their wounds incrementally.

This is a much more loving way to react to resistance. In much the same way you wouldn't force a scared child to talk before he's ready, it is kind to let your mind work at its own pace. By giving the mind permission to heal one piece at a time, you can lower the pressure about doing it all now. Sometimes this lets the walls down and enables a surprising amount of work to happen.

Remember, if you have dissociation symptoms as described in chapter 5 in the warning section, or if you can barely keep your emotions together in everyday life, you might need to start more slowly and with support. There is nothing wrong with this: knowing where you are on the journey will help you decide where to start.

2. Focus on the fear of feeling instead of the feeling itself.

When your emotions are scary enough that your mind would yell, "No way, I can't handle that!" there will be mental layers of protection. For example, should the hurt feel so deep that if you touch it, you will break, there will be a layer of fear keeping you from that hurt.

This comes up regularly when I work with clients. Make no mistake, the idea that a feeling will break someone is an actual fear. I've heard people say—and believe—the following:

- "If I feel all of that, it will break me."

- "If I start crying, I'll never stop."

- "I'm afraid that if I go there, I'll go crazy. I'll need to be locked up."

- "If I let the anger come up, I'm afraid I'll hurt someone."

- "If I let those feelings come up, I won't be able to function. I'll lose everything."

These are no small fears. Some people have had periods when they couldn't function due to overwhelming emotions. To feel without wallowing in despair or becoming engulfed in emotion can be a tricky skill to learn and might happen a little at a time. Consider this case:

Manuel smoked marijuana anytime he was conscious and not working. At work, he barely got through the day's anxiety using his prescriptions. He smoked before work and the moment he got home.

When we first tried therapeutic mindfulness, Manuel felt anxiety but also noticed deep sadness in his stomach. Manuel described the sadness as a blue, cold, heavy feeling that felt "as large as a building." When I had him focus on the sadness, his anxiety intensified into fear.

Because his fear eclipsed the sadness, I asked him to focus on the fear of feeling. Manuel said his fear was "as heavy as an elephant" on his chest, blue and hot, constricting his breathing. This is where we focused for the rest of the session.

As therapy progressed, I noticed that every subject we discussed brought up anxiety. Manuel had avoided emotions so completely for so long that he had become afraid of feeling anything! In therapy, we began to slowly address the fear.

Feelings that seem overwhelming have layers of protection to help us function. Fear is a common protective layer. Remember with Manuel, the fear eclipsed sadness that was already the size of a building. That's a lot of emotion! When people feel this kind of intensity, it is best to work with a therapist. A soothing person can help you regulate your feelings.

If you believe you can tackle the fear on your own and you have a good support system, you can use therapeutic mindfulness. When the fear of feeling becomes stronger than the feeling, simply focus on the fear. I help people create the target for therapeutic mindfulness by asking, "What if you let all of the feeling come up right now? Does that bring up fear?"

They typically answer with an emphatic yes. I go right to step 2 of therapeutic mindfulness by asking, "If the fear was somewhere in your body, where would you feel it the most? If the fear had a size, how big would it be? If it had a color, what would that be?" etcetera.

There are times when the fear takes quite a while to heal, but very often its reign of terror is surprisingly short-lived. Mind you, the fear is extremely uncomfortable, but then it goes away, sometimes within fifteen minutes. Once a client focuses on and allows the fear, it changes, then dissolves. After this happens, they can address the sadness or hurt that lies underneath the fear.

When the fear is gone, I ask clients whether they'd be willing to feel the feeling. They shrug and say, "Sure." They know it will be uncomfortable, but that no longer scares them. It's almost funny to see that nonchalant reaction when twenty minutes earlier, they were completely freaked out. What a difference!

3. Focus on the emotional layers of protection around the feeling instead of the feeling.

The mind has many ways to protect you from hidden feelings and beliefs. When using therapeutic mindfulness, focus without judgment on whatever experience is at the surface.

Minh was a young Asian-American woman who had a feeling that was stuck and wanted to stay stuck. It would not move or change as she observed it in her body, so I asked her a question I use to get past blocked feelings: "Notice the part of the feeling that is stuck. We can't force that part to go away, and we don't want to. We never try to force a feeling to do something. But we are going to do a what-if scenario. *Without pushing this feeling away, I want to see if you can peek behind it. Ask yourself, 'If this stuck part was not there, what would be behind it?'*"

Typically, peeking behind a block reveals overwhelming feelings like fear, as discussed in the last section. However, Minh said, "I would feel happy. I would be able to love my parents the way I want to." Minh's statement implied that something was getting in the way of her better loving her parents. The block wasn't hiding happiness. There was something else keeping her from that love she wanted. I gently suggested she look at both positive and negative feelings behind the block. This created a major change.

"I feel some anger. I didn't know it was there." As I continued to have her explore, she said, "I think I'm angry at my parents." As she continued being with the emotions in her body, Minh noticed that she held a lot of anger. When we discussed her experience afterward, she shared that not only was anger unacceptable in her family, but anger at one's parents was taboo in her culture.

Because she could not acknowledge her anger, Minh was holding onto it. This anger was stuffed down, but it flared up at each hurtful interaction with her parents. Minh felt unheard and unloved, helpless and depressed. She tried to ignore her hurt feelings so she could have a relationship, especially with her mother, and instead, she spent periods of time not speaking with her family at all.

Minh's family did not seem abusive or mean. Rather, they struggled with communication, defensiveness, and hurt feelings. I gently suggested that she could still observe her culture by behaving respectfully to her parents and that acknowledging the anger in therapy gave her the chance to work through it. If she was able to do that, she would not be so hurt during these interactions with her mother and might be able to connect more effectively.

I was careful to ensure that Minh felt comfortable that we would not be violating her cultural mandates by working with the anger. Only with her consent did we more closely explore this issue.

This case illustrates how deep beliefs can create barriers to addressing feelings. In this case, it was imperative in Minh's culture to respect one's parents, and for some, that means not holding anger. Yet we can't simply stop the anger: We can only hide it. Minh's anger was buried, and yet it would surface to hurt her relationship with her parents again and again.

Minh needed to learn not to judge herself for having anger and to understand that she could work through the anger internally without behaving disrespectfully toward her family. As she came to trust the process, her mind could do more healing work.

A judgment that a feeling is not acceptable can push it out of our awareness. Imagery like a wall or dam can show up when trying to get to emotions. Whenever you feel stuck or blocked, you can ask the stuck part, "If I could peek behind this stuck feeling, what would I see behind it?"

When trying this question, listen to how much vulnerability your mind is ready for in that moment, and don't push. Be gentle with your mind in the process. If you simply learn there is an ocean of feeling underneath a block, that's okay. Feelings are information. You can take that information to your support system or your therapist. You can also continue to be aware of it as you work on your growth. When it is ready, it will allow you to peek behind it and start the healing process.

4. Focus on physical layers of protection around the feeling instead of the feeling.

Blocks can come up as physical symptoms. I've had clients experience the following:

- Headache

- Dizziness

- Feeling sick or nauseous

- Muscle pain or soreness

- Feeling too warm

If you notice physical symptoms pop up the moment you have strong emotions, one option is to shift your focus to the physical discomfort. If the physical feeling is the strongest part of your experience, try this approach.

Many times, I've had clients with no headache or nausea suddenly develop the symptoms once we started working with emotions. That's a clue. They usually say something like, "Perhaps I'm dehydrated," or, "My allergies are kicking in."

Here are two cases of emotions becoming physical symptoms:

> Joe told me, "I'm hot, but I'm wearing this thick sweatshirt." He insisted this was the reason even though I asked whether he was hot before the session started and he had said, "No." I had him continue therapeutic mindfulness while noticing the sense of being hot. As is common, his physical symptoms went away within ten minutes.

*

> Mark was the client who got dizzy when dealing with any difficult emotions. With practice, he eventually learned to face his feelings head-on. My first clue that I had hit a nerve was always a yawn. On one occasion after he'd been in my office for thirty-five minutes, I brought up a difficult subject, and he suddenly started yawning—he yawned three times within ninety seconds! When I pointed this out, he insisted he was sleepy. I playfully mentioned that he only got sleepy after I brought up the subject.

It took years of giving him these gentle examples before he accepted this lifelong pattern. Once, during some deep emotional work, Mark recognized the physical sensations are the same as when he's had concussions. His body would create that feeling when he got emotional, and he would then find the nearest place to pass out. He told me he would wake up with a wet face and not know why it was wet.

Through facing feelings, he built resilience, and these symptoms occurred less often and less intensely. When they did come up strongly, I would have him focus on the dizziness, the tiredness, or how much he wanted to sleep. I might ask him, "Right now, how badly do you want to sleep? Notice that feeling."

For the record, he never actually fell asleep in my office, contrary to his many threats that this would happen if he focused on the desire to sleep. Recently he told me he used to sleep after each session with me. He has evolved. He now says that he feels relief after we do emotional work.

These examples show how vivid physical sensations can be even if they appear to have nothing to do with the emotions. In Mark's case, the strong desire to sleep seems to exist to distract from the uncomfortable emotion.

In another example, I had a client whose bouts of nausea and exhaustion would come and then pass within thirty minutes of therapeutic mindfulness. Anything that comes up more strongly than the initial feeling should become your focus. These layers exist to protect your vulnerable parts. They should not be a source of shame or self-loathing. It is very healing for them to be given the care and attention they deserve.

As you work with whatever comes up, those protective layers fall away, and you get closer to the vulnerable parts. As those parts heal, you become strong, resilient, and unafraid.

5. Work with your anger.

Anger might show up in different ways. At first, I suggest you use the standard process of therapeutic mindfulness. This might work, but anger can be tricky because it often comes with judgment. Anger could feel very justified, or there could be a belief that you need the anger. Anger could be unacceptable and tied in with self-judgment. If your anger doesn't get better, here are some things to try.

When the anger is stuck, one option is the same strategy we used with fear. There is likely a feeling beneath the anger that is being protected. Because anger feels so different from fear, I will highlight what it looks like to work with anger.

First, acknowledge the anger. Then you can gently try to peek behind it. I might prompt a client in this way: "We cannot and do not want to force any feeling to go away, but just for now, let's be curious. What if the anger were not there? Can you peek behind it and see what else is there?"

This exploration might lead to strong feelings of fear or hurt. Whatever comes up most strongly is the new focus. Continue to work through the feelings as much as your mind feels it is ready for that day. If there is fear of the feeling, then sit with the fear. You might need to revisit strategy #2 from this chapter. Remember that layers of protection are normal and healing them one at a time gets you closer to healing the core. Stay open to listening to yourself about your need to lean on a support such as friends or a therapist.

There is also another option for working with anger. After describing the feeling in your body using the body focusing questions, speak to the anger as a hurt part. Tell the anger that you can see how hard it is to be the anger. It is hard to be the part that needs to stand up and protect, to always be strong and never let its guard down. It's hard to have so much responsibility. I bet it feels tiring to be the anger, but the anger never gets to rest. Notice the anger with these thoughts or talk directly to it. Remember not to try to change it. Just be with it and share these thoughts of understanding. You can also say to it, "I can see this is hard, but you don't have to do it alone. I'm here."

These thoughts are gentle and without judgment and can create a breakthrough for part of you that never had a chance to feel listened to and understood.

6. Watch out for the trap of "Why?"

Just today (at the time of this writing), I had yet another person tell me that their goal in therapy was to figure out why they feel as they do. I usually ask, "If you knew why, would you feel better?"

In her case, she had an intellectual understanding that her childhood trauma was impacting her self-esteem and trust issues. I agreed but pointed out that her understanding has not fixed her emotions.

Needing an answer to "Why?" is a distraction at best—and a judgment at worst. Consider Laura's story:

> Laura often got caught up on the question "why?" when trying to work through emotions. Her mind focused on asking, "Why?" so much so that it sidelined her efforts. She would say, "I know I feel better when I'm calm. Why do I keep getting caught up in anxiety?" or, "Why can't I just let go?"
>
> In her early attempts to use mindfulness, she always got sidetracked. She noticed confusion or sometimes frustration. I thought her asking, "Why?" might indicate pity, as if asking, "Why me?"
>
> One day as we were exploring, I realized this was *not* the case. There was neither confusion nor self-pity. It was self-judgment. That's where the frustration came in. That's why things never got better for her. The word "why" was irrelevant in her case. To see what she was truly saying, just remove that word. "Why can't I just let go?" becomes the harsh statement, "I can't let go," as if to say, "I can't let go, and I'm such an idiot that I deserve to be in pain." The statement, "Why do I keep getting caught up in anxiety?" meant, "I keep getting caught up in anxiety even though I know better. I'm so stupid because I clearly can't do this right. I'll never be better and it's my fault. I'm hopeless."
>
> In her case, "Why?" is not a question. It is condemnation.
>
> When I shared this new interpretation, Laura immediately recognized her harsh inner critic. I had her notice the judgment but then allow herself to feel in her body anyway. I instructed her not to worry about why. When the questions would come, I suggested she go in with compassion and acceptance towards herself instead.
>
> Laura focused on her body sensations, and after a time I asked her what she noticed. She had started to calm down at first, but then her anxiety got worse again. Her inner voice was supposed to be supportive, saying,

"I've been through a lot and it's okay for me to feel anxious," and, "I've had a really hard time, so I'm allowed to feel this."

If she was being supportive, why was her anxiety going up again?

I immediately saw the problem and instructed her to try again, but this time to *not* justify her anxiety. If her mind asked, "Why do I feel anxious?" I suggested she respond by saying, "It doesn't matter why, I just do." Rather than focusing on justification, this statement was designed to get her focused on accepting that she felt bad.

Remember, *allowing* is key.

Laura tried this for a while, repeating that phrase to herself as necessary and staying with the feeling. When I checked in, she had quickly become calmer and more peaceful than she had been in quite a while.

I explained to Laura the problem with justifying her anxiety. If we need to justify our feelings, it means that part of us believes we should not have them. We're trying to talk ourselves out of feeling, and our other part fights back.

When we accept our experience, we don't have to argue about why it's okay to feel anxious. The justifying part says, "I should get to feel this way, honestly, really, and truly, and golly, will you please agree so I can let myself feel this way?"

Once Laura began justifying, her jerk brain predictably gave responses like, "What's the matter with you? You think that's so bad? Others have had it worse. What a wimp!" *This* was when her anxiety started shooting up again.

We must learn to nurture our hurt parts the way we would a child. If a three-year-old girl is shaking visibly with terror, we don't ask, "Why?" then wait for the little one to justify her fear, and then if and only if we agree that she has sufficient reason to be scared, we comfort her!

We know this is not how to nurture a child, yet as adults, we believe we must justify our feelings or else we're weak and stupid. The solution is simply to accept and nurture it. Once the feeling is soothed, we quickly return to a high-functioning state of mind.

If you're working with your emotions and you get the intrusive question of "Why?" you can gently remind yourself, "It doesn't matter why. This *is* how I feel." Focus on the fact of the feeling. If you want to give the feeling extra nurturing, notice that it's hard to be an anxious, sad, angry, or hurt feeling. Then return to observing the feeling.

Ironically, you sometimes get spontaneous insights about "why" after a feeling starts to heal. But either way, when the feeling is completely healed, you will find the "why" no longer matters.

7. Don't let the urge to act get you off track from fixing the feeling.

There are times that your ways of adapting might distract you from addressing the actual problem. Of course, this is no accident.

The *urge to act* is a strong distraction. We sometimes feel we cannot be happy until we act. This could be related to strong anxiety or anger. The urge itself is a powerful subject for therapeutic mindfulness.

One simple trick is to give yourself permission to act in any way you feel is important . . . later! You may act *after* the feeling is healed, but for right now, you are going to work on the feeling. Once you are calm, your actions will come from a clear-headed place.

Here's an example of the *urge to placate*:

> Brandon's family was conditioned to cater to his mother's emotional outbursts. As an adult, this deeply engrained habit took shape in his relationships. When a romantic partner became angry, his anxiety would skyrocket, and he would not relax until he successfully placated his partner. This happened even if he knew she was controlling or cruel. For Brandon, his perceived guilt and the threat of abandonment were far too overwhelming for him to stand up for himself, even when he realized she was not a good match for him.

I recently had another client who is also unable to leave a controlling relationship for the same reason. Sadly, this is common. For Brandon, we worked on his guilt and fear of loss. After these emotions resolved themselves, he was able to choose the first loving and equitable relationship of his life.

Let's look at the *urge to fix*:

Alex was a problem solver. She had a decades-long habit of over-functioning to address her family's needs. She facilitated all things, from parenting when her husband was drunk, to coordinating events (including holidays) with her extended in-laws, to finding any and all resources for life changes (including moving to a new city), to helping her teen through a suicidal time. Her swift and effective action was truly something to behold.

And yet Alex's over-functioning kept her husband from experiencing any negative consequences stemming from his immaturity. In a common codependent pattern, she held all the stress and responsibility of running their lives while he drank comfortably.

A central issue was how Alex expended great energy attempting to fix her husband's unhealthy attitudes and relationships with all her children and herself, to no avail. He had no reason to change. She was the only motivated party.

When Alex's husband and children fought, I suggested that instead of jumping into the argument, trying to convince him of his misdeeds—a tactic which had not worked over the years—she pause and mindfully observe her desire to jump in and change things.

Keep in mind that the purpose of this exercise was not for Alex to give up on change in general. In her case, trying to create change in her marriage hadn't worked and she was stuck in an endless loop. Alex was so focused on action that she couldn't see the patterns or understand her emotional urge to jump in. Just observing could potentially help her see whether there was another option.

Alex did just this. When she wanted to fix the arguments and control the situation, she instead watched the scenes play out. She then used therapeutic mindfulness to sit with her desire to join the argument. This enabled her to see her family's patterns more clearly when she did not give in to her urge to fix.

Over a three-week period, she began to realize that her urge to fix the problem meant that she was taking responsibility upon herself to fix the emotionally abusive relationship her husband had with their children. Deep down she believed she could fix it, change it, if only she tried hard enough or found the right approach. By stepping back, she realized that there had been no improvements in decades. Moreover, trying to make him change kept her engaged in the marriage with her endless and fruitless problem-solving. After more than twenty years of trying, she realized that changing him was truly a battle she could not win.

Working through the urge to fix was the first step to understanding the patterns of emotional abuse and control. Alex saw how her husband was able to keep her around as long as she thought she could change him because she still had skin in the game.

Observing rather than *reacting* opened the door to new information. Eventually, it became clear that she wanted to free herself and her children from a home life of control and manipulation. Within a few months, she gained the strength to ask him to leave the home and seek professional help.

The irony in Alex's story was that she was so incredibly capable, and yet her resourcefulness was used against her to keep a bad situation going. It brings to mind the serenity prayer and the importance of having the wisdom to know the difference between things one can and cannot change.

By using therapeutic mindfulness focused on her urge to fix, Alex was able to overcome the urge and gain insight into her relationship patterns, leading to a life more in line with her values.

If you feel a strong urge to act, you can describe it in your body and use therapeutic mindfulness. After working through a feeling, you can still choose to act—or not—using the wisdom you have deep inside you. Once your jerk brain is no longer active, you have access to your *higher self*. Life becomes calmer when you act from a place of wisdom rather than a place of fear and compulsion.

When dealing with the urge to act, you also have the opportunity to explore the core beliefs at play. In Alex's case, these were: "I am responsible," and "I need to fix/save the situation." Stepping away from the beliefs that control you and working through the related emotions will free you to be in control of yourself.

Another distraction would be the compulsion to have someone else fix your feelings rather than sitting with them.

Consider the *urge to seek reassurance*:

> Jane had a chronic and obsessive fear of losing her job. Whenever an uncomfortable interaction would occur at work, whether it be an email or a comment from a coworker, Jane would compulsively go to her boss to seek reassurance that her job was safe. Jane would also endlessly complain to her mother, her spouse, and her friends, all of whom attempted to help.

> Their reassurance sometimes soothed her briefly until the next negative thought spiral or micro-interaction. Everyone in her support system eventually got frustrated with Jane's repetitive and irrational fears. At times, Jane would share how she was hurt when her mother, spouse, and even her boss lashed out at her needy appeals.

> Jane needed to look at her urge to seek reassurance. I helped Jane explore her core belief. Deep down, she believed, "I'm helpless." Over time, Jane began to see how different triggers all tied back to this fear, even from a time when she was too young to have a job.

> In recognizing this, Jane understood that the problem was not the job, it was the core belief. When she got the urge to seek reassurance, we started working with the helpless part of her in a compassionate way.

In general, sharing your anxieties with friends and family is a good way to get perspective. Discussing concerns with a spouse can help with problems and deepen intimacy.

Support helps, but the responsibility for your feelings is ultimately yours. When you find the same things coming up time after time, that's your clue that there's a deeper issue to fix. We don't have to walk our life journey alone, nor should we. Others can walk beside us, but we get nowhere unless we actually walk.

The bottom line remains the same for Jane as it did for Alex. When we have a strong desire to act on something, we can work through the urge to act. There might be a lot there to heal. You will likely find emotions or core beliefs underneath that urge. The urge is a distraction: it's the hurt parts feeding it that need your help.

If you don't have a compulsive urge to act, you will not lose your survival instinct, or your wisdom about when to act. In fact, your head will be clearer and your decisions more solid.

The exercise below is one way to gauge whether your actions are fear-based or wise.

Exercise 8: Using Your Higher Self for Decisions

1. Choose a decision for which you want clarification.

2. Create a calm mental state. You can do this with meditation or breathing exercises. (If you're not used to doing this on your own, try a meditation from an app or look up "guided meditation" on YouTube. There are many methods for how to get into a calm mental state. Find one that works for you.)

3. Verify that your mind is calm (your thinking feels slow and relaxed) and that your feelings are calm.

4. Check in on the decision you were considering. Is this decision coming from a place of calm or a place of turmoil (usually fear)?

5. Ask yourself: "If my mind was perfectly at ease, would this be my decision?"

6. Listen for the answer. You will feel whether that decision draws you in or makes you want to pull away.

This simple exercise tells you whether you are responding out of fear or wisdom. I believe we absolutely have the wisdom we need, but we can only access it when our thoughts and emotions are quiet. If fear guides your decision, following that decision teaches your mind to live a fear-based life. You can learn to trust your wisdom when you *practice* making decisions based on your higher self. Once the mind is calm, that inner voice becomes clear.

I have mentioned the advantages of getting professional help if you get stuck or overwhelmed. This is because the focus of the chapter is what happens when subconscious protections come up to block progress. We all have some resistance, which serves as protection for the hurt and vulnerable parts of us. You might well be able to work past them using the tips in this chapter, but some people have very powerful protections in place for a reason. There is no shame in getting extra support.

Whether or not you need extra help in specific areas that won't budge, the general practice of therapeutic mindfulness will build your tolerance for discomfort and lower your judgmental tendencies. You can always start small and work your way up. The benefits are well worth the effort.

After reading through this chapter, can you see ways it relates to you? Beware the trap of exploring these tendencies in others! Analyzing others is one of the most compelling mind tricks of avoidance. I suggest you dedicate minimal time to this. Instead, consider the ways your personal resistance shows up. As you work through these layers of resistance, they will evolve. You will also develop deeper self-awareness as your work continues.

Remember, if you're making some progress, you're doing the work. Do not focus on being finished and completely healed. The goal is not for you to be perfect; it's for you to be happy. Perfection is a trick to hide the belief that our mistakes mean we are fundamentally bad or unlovable. Happiness comes more freely when we accept that we can mess up yet still be worthy of receiving love and capable of giving love.

Chapter Twelve

MEASURING PROGRESS

L et's say you've been doing therapeutic mindfulness for a while. Perhaps you are working through emotional reactions that have been in place for decades. This could be a tendency to get angry, defensive, fearful, or down on yourself. You want to change these reactions. After a lot of work, you think you've beaten it. You've stopped reacting. Then something happens and the same old pattern plays out all over again.

I know this is extremely frustrating but let me prepare you now for this eventuality. Healing is not like turning off a light switch. During times of intense stress, old reactions are likely to resurface. This is normal. It happens to us all. You might wonder: "If it comes back, how do I know I've made progress?"

Checking Your Goals

Short-Term Progress

Healing is not a dramatic movie climax in which the main character is suddenly transformed. Rather, it is realistic, reliable, and reproducible. The process is more like peeling layers off an onion. We heal one layer at a time. When a layer comes off, it might still make you cry, but it's smaller and continues to get smaller until it no longer affects you.

Hopefully, by now you've been practicing and are seeing results on specific targets. It feels great to get past the pain of something. After doing therapeutic mindfulness, remember to return to the target and ask, "When you think of [the target], how much emotion comes back?" If some emotion comes back, continue the process (describe and allow) until the feeling is resolved.

Checking back can show just how much a feeling has changed. I always chuckle when a person says, as if with a shrug, "It happened. It's in the past." Sometimes it seems like they are saying, "Why bring that up? It's yesterday's news." I will remind them that just mentioning the subject left them crippled with emotion 30 minutes earlier. Some people are surprised when they realize their reaction could change so quickly using therapeutic mindfulness.

More commonly, the target is improved but there is still work to be done. In these cases, I'll check on the intensity of the target and hear something like: "It's as big as a quarter," when the feeling started out as big as a softball.

If you like more concrete comparisons, you can use a pain scale. If anxiety was rated on a scale of 1–10, with 10 being the worst anxiety possible, how intense was it at the start? Although this is not a perfect measurement, most people have an impression of an answer. For example, someone will say that the anxiety started at an 8 but is now a 4. That's a very noticeable difference! In this case, the process is working, but they could do more work and bring it down to a 2 or less.

If you attempt therapeutic mindfulness, only to see that the target triggered strong emotion all over again, you might have been avoiding the pain of it or trying to *make* it calm down. Therapeutic mindfulness is not about calming; it is about healing. If the feeling is healed, you will no longer need to use coping skills to calm it.

If you find all the emotion still comes up when you think of a target, return to the allowing phrases. It can be especially helpful for you to invite the feeling to get bigger or worse. Then focus on allowing yourself to be with all of the feeling. It cannot heal if it is in hiding.

Another way to catch avoidance is to ask yourself afterward: "Is there anything I avoided?" You will intuitively know the answer.

The bottom line is that you've made progress if the target is less painful than when you started. You can really celebrate when the target feels about as painful as describing the color of paint on a wall.

Long-Term Progress

If you are working on deep feelings that have plagued you for many years, you are in for a slow-and-steady climb toward a healthier you. Here are common examples of long-term issues:

1. Self-esteem – Self-esteem appears to be deeply woven into the personality. It can shift, but it takes time and deep, consistent emotional work.

2. Patterns of controlling or abusive relationships – Whether you can be abusive, are being abused, or both, this is very often connected to self-esteem and can shift over time with deep, consistent emotional work.

3. Phobias – I have not used this method with simple phobias like spiders or elevators. Phobias such as agoraphobia or emetophobia are often rooted in deep trauma with heavy layers of protection. This is a slow road and is likely to require professional help. I recommend finding a therapist who is trained in EMDR and well-versed in working with trauma. EMDR and therapeutic mindfulness are complementary therapies.

4. Anger issues – People struggling with difficulty controlling anger outbursts likely have a pattern of avoidance and protection. This relates to an intense fear of vulnerability and reluctance to face painful things. It might take a while to get used to this work. With persistence, it is possible to improve.

5. Dissociation – People who tend to space out or get dizzy or sleepy might need to work through their avoidance and fear. When you're able to catch this pattern and keep yourself present, you might be able to use therapeutic mindfulness successfully on your own. If you are unable to catch yourself starting to dissociate, or if you have more dramatic symptoms like blocking recent events and losing time (see the warning section in chapter 5), work with a therapist who specializes in trauma and dissociation.

6. Difficulty being alone – This refers to relationship hopping that comes from the need to be in a relationship. I have seen this improve in less than a year, of course depending on the severity and amount of work done.

Even when working on long-term issues, you can check your short-term targets. For example, if you deal with anger and you're able to think of a specific situation that gets you angry every time, use that as a target for therapeutic mindfulness. You can check at the end whether that trigger has changed. As you work through multiple short-term targets, the underlying core beliefs shift, leading to long-term change.

It's normal to want to see evidence that your efforts are having a greater effect on you and your life. Journaling can provide perspective on your progress. For some, it is helpful to write down situations that trigger you, how you react, and what you'd like to change. The "Progress Tracker" lays out the many facets with which you react when triggered (see the Appendix). You can use the progress tracker as a worksheet or as a freestyle writing prompt. Some people like to journal after a session of therapeutic mindfulness to record insights and new ideas.

If you've been practicing and journaling, or reflecting on your journey, how do you measure progress?

Therapists measure growth by the duration (D), intensity (I), and frequency (F) of symptoms, or DIF. Review the DIF if you want to check for DIF-ferences!

Duration (D):

> Amelia described having intense spirals of despair that lasted for days. During one session, she shared being triggered over the weekend. As was common, her despair left her immobile on the floor all night. She spent the following day exhausted in bed. I suggested she try using therapeutic mindfulness, as she had been practicing successfully at home. Because it was not yet a habit, I suggested she leave her handouts for body focusing questions and allowing phrases on her nightstand as a reminder.

> A few weeks later the same thing happened—a trigger began a spiral of despair. Amelia saw the handouts on her bedside and decided to use them. She worked through her intense feelings in thirty minutes! Later that evening, another wave of emotion hit her. She dove right back in and, this time found resolution in ten minutes. After that, her weekend was calm and normal. Forty minutes is a definite improvement from a day and a half!

Intensity (I):

Carrie had been dating her on-again, off-again boyfriend for six years. She was often dissatisfied with the relationship and said she was an "idiot" for staying. Yet when she tried to stop dating him, she would panic. She believed that no one would ever want her again.

Their fights were frequent and predictable. He would blow up over something like her turning down a date, and he would try to pull her into the fight. She would yell and scream or try to defend herself. If she wouldn't fight, he would fly into a rage, obsessively texting nasty messages for days. Sometimes she would block him, so he would blast her on social media. Sooner or later, she would get drawn into the battle.

Even when she got angry at his behavior, the guilt weighed on her. She told me, "I had gnawing self-doubt that I didn't give enough. Maybe if I was less something . . . less selfish or less emotional, this wouldn't have happened." The intensity of the guilt would wear her out until she was sobbing and desperate for reassurance. Then she said, "He would collect me and hold me. It would be so comforting. Then he would say how he would change his behavior, talk about how much better he would be and promise all of these things."

Because Carrie's pattern began long before this boyfriend, we worked on her underlying core belief, "I am unlovable." As therapy progressed, Carrie was able to see the pattern of fight, break up, and make-up that checkered their relationship. She started setting boundaries and attempted to stop the old habits. She noticed, "It would take longer to draw me into the fights, and it would take harsher things." She started noticing that insecurities she had confided in him about would later be used against her, more and more harshly. Sometimes she would be able to resist. She told me about several fights where she stayed calm until he eventually apologized. At other times, her jerk brain outweighed her new way of thinking and the old habits would take over.

As her work continued, Carrie noticed she no longer felt panic when he was upset with her. She told me, "Before I would have a grumpy day and I would blame myself. About a month ago, I had a grumpy day, and he was mad at me for it. He started a fight. I was removed enough to notice that it was all him and that I'm allowed to have a bad mood. If he can't accept that, then I don't need to accept his behavior."

During this fight, her jerk brain was still active, but Carrie said, "It was quieter. It didn't hit the same emotionally." Because her emotions were so much calmer, Carrie could make decisions without fear of repercussions. When he got upset, the twinge of guilt she felt was mild enough not to override her logical mind.

At the time of this interview, there had been another fight. Carrie said, "The whole thing looked ridiculous. He got more intense to draw me in. It does affect me to be verbally abused, and I cried, but he had to do that because I wasn't getting drawn in." Carrie blocked him to stop the torrent of hostility. She then thought of the things that would always bring back her longing for him. She told me, "The pang of missing him was gone." Her old negative core belief, "No one else will love me," was at zero percent. She felt content to appreciate her current relationships with her children, friends, and pets.

Carrie's story shows how the intensity of her guilt and panic lessened over the course of eleven months until she no longer felt the need to react. She didn't get there instantly, but I remember her sharing times when she fought back and other times when she was able to stay calm and observe the fight while keeping her boundaries. As we kept working through her core beliefs, she shared more often how old things just didn't hook her the way they once had.

Frequency (F):

If a client tells me they have panic attacks three times a week, the initial goal is to lessen the frequency of the panic attacks. When the client has a panic attack, it still might be just as upsetting—perhaps even more so if it had been a while and the client hoped they were "cured." However, going from three panic attacks each week to two panic attacks in the past month is a great improvement.

When you question your progress, look at the past. Clients find great relief when I remind them where they were six months, a year, or two years ago. I remind them how easily or often they were triggered, how intensely they reacted, or how difficult things were. When they think back, it's easy to see the change. They become gentler to themselves, and their hope renews.

To measure progress, it helps to explore details about how you reacted in the past compared to now. When working on your own, this is where reviewing journal entries can be useful.

For example, if violent thoughts have become irritated thoughts, that's progress in thoughts. If fear has become discomfort, that's progress in emotions. If blowing up at a family member or subordinate becomes grumbling passive-aggressively, that's still progress in behavior. If emotions presented as stabbing neck or shoulder pain have become muscle tension, that's progress in body reactions. As you can see, intensity of symptoms can be checked on the level of thought, emotion, behavior, and physical (body) reactions.

If you use core beliefs when doing therapeutic mindfulness, you can check the intensity of the core belief by asking yourself, "What percentage of me *believes* the core belief?" (Belief refers to emotional belief, not logical belief.)

For example, if the core belief, "I'm not good enough," comes up for you repeatedly, ask yourself what percentage of you believes this is true. This isn't about what you think. You might think that you are good enough logically, but if you check deep down, you don't buy it. Or you might feel confident in general until a certain target comes up. Then suddenly your negative core belief is activated. One client recently told me that 50 percent of her believed she was worthless after feeling triggered. This might sound bad, but when we first met, that number was 95 percent. Her belief in her worth rose from 5 percent to 50 percent.

Progress is neither euphoria nor perfection. It merely means that you spend more time feeling like yourself instead of being emotionally reactive or "all in your feels." When you react to problems, you will still feel uncomfortable. When I have clients look back to where they started, they often comment that they would certainly not want to go backward! Journaling or some form of progress tracking will help you see your journey more clearly and keep you motivated to work on yourself.

As you consider your progress, remember that growth is a process. A healthy mindset accepts where you are in the process of change.

Fear of Relapse

I've seen it all too often. A client is making great progress. He goes weeks or months without the strong feelings that used to plague him weekly or even daily. He is doing great. He is ready to move on or tackle other problems.

Then it happens. He gets triggered. Perhaps it's a fight with a romantic partner or a call from a parent. Perhaps it's a tragic event. The old feelings rush back. This should not shake him, right? After all, he used to live with these feelings all the time. But good ol' jerk brain spins a scary story and it sounds like this:

> "I thought I'd made all this progress. I thought I was really changing. I've been going to therapy and facing my feelings. I did what I'm supposed to do, and now I'm right back to where I started! I've worked so hard, and now all that work is down the drain. This proves what a failure I am. I'll never get better. It's hopeless. I'm hopeless."

I've seen how the despair comes not from the incident, nor the feelings, but from the fear that one cannot heal. This simply isn't true—and the despair can pass very quickly by looking back a year and seeing the progress. That's why journaling is so helpful. It gives a perspective that is much needed during temporary setbacks. Consider this story:

> Zoe came to see me because of intense defensiveness that caused battles with her boyfriend every two or three days. She had been working hard, and things had been going well. One day she came in very upset and blaming herself harshly.

"I thought I was better. Last night we had this big fight and I was right back to where I used to be, defensive and angry. He was close to leaving me before. Now I'm worried that I can't change and I'll lose him."

I asked Zoe to recall how often they used to fight due to her defensiveness. She tearfully recalled fighting several times a week. I asked how long it had been since their last big fight. She thought about it and said in wonderment, "Five weeks ago."

Zoe was astonished by the difference, and her hope was restored. When she had the next blow-up a few months later, she was able to see the changes in her relationship quality. Understanding her incremental progress helped her flow with future setbacks and keep her eyes on the big picture.

Jerk brain loves to trick us into thinking our work is futile and to get us back into our cycle of hopelessness. Yet if you had to choose between fights in your relationship thrice weekly or once every few months, the choice is clear. If you had to choose between daily panic attacks or monthly panic attacks, again, the choice is clear.

Another trick is to write a letter to the triggered version of you at a time when you feel calm. You might keep it somewhere very accessible, like the top drawer of your nightstand. You could keep it in an envelope and label it with something like, "In case of emergency, open me." Using your higher mind perspective, you might find that you know exactly what you need to hear when triggered to remember your progress and restore hope.

Change is a process. When we accept the lows with grace, it helps the process move along more smoothly because we're teaching ourselves to pause before reacting and to be kind to ourselves when we're not perfect.

A long-time client, Richard, reported being in a far better mood than he'd been in for many years. When his mood dipped, he reported it with great concern. He said the low mood persisted for three days and he feared relapsing into depression.

Because he'd been depressed for so long, that was all he knew. I explained that people who are not continually depressed do have ups and downs. I suggested he try to ride the wave, meaning to flow with the ups and downs. The next time his mood dipped, he remembered not to panic. This time his lower mood lasted for one day instead of three.

Over time, the less you react to jerk brain's antics, the less often they are used. Eventually, jerk brain will give up old tactics. This principle reminds me of a child who used to be able to get candy by throwing tantrums. If Mom learns to stop reacting to the tantrums by giving in, the child doesn't stop immediately, but over time the behavior fades away. The fits come less frequently. Eventually, the child learns that the approach no longer works. Jerk brain is that child.

One day you will hopefully realize that you're no longer as worked up by jerk brain's old tricks but that life is not perfect. Don't worry about perfection—since perfection is a unicorn (it doesn't exist). The payoff is spending more time feeling good, having better relationships, and making decisions with a clear mind. At some point, even more benefits come when you find you can help other people be happier. And if you listen to your higher self, it will steer your life in the right direction.

Other Types of Progress

We've talked about how to measure short-term and long-term progress on specific goals. Your goal might be to change how you react to a specific memory or situation. Or you might want to change the general habit of reacting with anxiety, anger, self-blame, etc. There are also other changes you might notice that come from habitually responding to your emotions using therapeutic mindfulness. If you've been practicing, take a moment to reflect on these questions:

1. Is it becoming easier to get out of your story and into your body's emotions?

2. Do you notice less fear or avoidance when preparing to face your emotions?

3. Are you able to detect more body sensations related to your experience than you used to?

4. Do you remember to use therapeutic mindfulness more quickly?

5. Do you sometimes feel eager to use therapeutic mindfulness, knowing the relief and calmness that can result? (Yes, some people become quite enthusiastic to jump in!)

6. Do you see situations that would have triggered you in the past and realize that you simply don't need to respond the way you used to?

7. Have you started watching your reactions to daily life from the perspective of a nonjudgmental observer?

8. Have you started thinking of yourself with more compassion?

The last two questions indicate that observing without judgment is becoming second nature. Can you imagine a life where you watch your reactions without judgment and habitually pause to be kind to yourself?

Practicing therapeutic mindfulness trains your mind to respond to emotions in a healthier way. Practitioners develop compassion, strength, and wisdom.

Exercise 9: Progress Questions

If you've decided to journal or log your reactions, these questions can help you gain awareness of key changes. Choose a time when you're feeling normal for you (not especially happy or upset, just a typical day) and answer these questions:

1. Right now, what percentage of my mind sees myself with compassion?

2. Right now, what percentage of my mind feels that I could emotionally handle a difficult situation were it to come up?

3. Do I see an improved ability to pause before reacting to an upsetting situation? (You might look back six months, or a year, etcetera.)

4. What percentage of me feels that I am growing?

5. If you have a specific core belief you're working on, bring up each one and ask: What percentage of my mind feels this negative core belief is true? What percentage of my mind believes that the opposite core belief is true? (i.e., "I am not good enough," becomes, "I am worthy as I am.")

Remember not to judge yourself for your answers. They provide information. If most of you believes a negative thing about yourself, that is useful information. It gives you a starting point from which to measure progress. This exercise can be useful, but do not force it. If you find yourself steeped in self-judgment, back away and focus on developing self-compassion. Above all, we must learn self-compassion to heal.

CHAPTER THIRTEEN

THERAPEUTIC MINDFULNESS – ADVANCED

If you've never done any type of mindfulness exercise, therapeutic mindfulness can be surprisingly powerful. Just know that nothing will replace experience. You could be in love with every idea presented in this book, but your understanding will be limited without practice. With experience, however, you gain more than I can describe.

Let's say you've been practicing therapeutic mindfulness and it's become second nature. You notice when you're triggered, find the upsetting thought, dive into the emotions of your body nonjudgmentally, and offer yourself compassion. If this is you, this chapter will make four suggestions that you might find helpful at times in your practice of therapeutic mindfulness.

Exploring a Story with Therapeutic Mindfulness

When you are new to using therapeutic mindfulness, I suggest keeping your focus on your body so you don't get caught up in jerk brain's story. If you find it easy to leave the story at will, you can use therapeutic mindfulness to explore a complicated memory or story and heal the hurts that arise. Mastering the mindfulness aspect of the practice—the *focus* and the *nonjudgment*—is the key. Once you're able to do this reliably, you can jump from your story to the body as needed.

Do you have a memory or an upsetting target that seems so complicated, it's hard to pick one thing to target? When this happens, you can start going through the memory or story. Notice your reaction as your jerk brain rambles on. Once you notice a spike of pain, stop! Get out of your story and into your body. It is time to use therapeutic mindfulness.

Sandy used this process when she was getting divorced:

> Sandy was driving to her former house to deal with some details of a divorce. She knew she would be facing her ex-husband-to-be. While driving, Sandy kept bursting into tears, which was not a good emotional state for such a meeting. She pulled into a parking lot. She did not need to find a trigger, as she could already feel strong emotions. She focused on her body using therapeutic mindfulness.

> Once the emotion had calmed, she returned to her thoughts and let jerk brain play out its story. It sounded something like this:

> *He seemed happy with me when we lived away from his family. Maybe it's because he doesn't make friends easily. Now that we live near his family, I'm not good enough. He's known me for ten years. He's always liked who I've been—well, at least in private. I thought he did, anyway. I was just good enough to keep him company in between his business trips, but now that I can't act like a Stepford robot wife, I don't fit in his life, which means it was all fake. I was just filler, and he never really loved me at all.*

> Once this last thought hit her, Sandy's throat clenched up. She was flooded with emotion.

> Because she hit a spike of emotion, she got out of the story and into her body, where progress can be made. (This is done by describing using the body focusing questions.) She focused completely on the physical sensations. She sat with a wave of hurt and sadness. She observed the feeling's contours and changes until it ebbed and she was completely calm. She revisited the thought that had triggered the strong emotion. "He never really loved me at all." She checked in with her body and

found no reaction. She was perfectly calm. It was just a thought that had happened, and now it held no pain. This healed, Sandy returned to her jerk brain's story to find the next trigger.

When we broke up, he said, "I just want you to be happy." I believed him. He sounded so sincere . . . until we started talking about money. Suddenly, he decided that I shouldn't get a share in our finances because I had earned less, even though I lost well-paying jobs multiple times by moving. I quit my job so he could keep the career he loved. He fawned over me at the time. Now, conveniently, my contribution means nothing to him. How dare he overlook that and treat me like I'm some possession and not an equal contributor in our life together! That's all I ever was, all I ever meant to him. He says he wants me to be happy but doesn't care if I'm poor in my old age—so long as he doesn't have to give up anything. Money means more to him than I ever did . . . I was just another possession, a convenience.

Sandy's throat clenched up. She was flooded with emotion. Sandy paused her story. Because she hit a spike of emotion, she got out of the story and returned to her body, where progress can be made. This time she felt anger, betrayal, and indignation. She focused completely on the physical sensations. She sat with the heat and the tension, describing and observing it as it rose and fell. She leaned into the discomfort, reminding herself to open up to it, to let it be there. The intensity of emotion washed over her. Eventually, it ebbed. Sandy revisited the triggering thought, "Money means more to him than I ever did." She noticed some irritation, but it was manageable. Sandy knew she would have to continue working on her resentment as it came up in different ways, but it seemed mild enough to keep her from reacting badly while seeing him face to face.

In this way, Sandy worked through one or two more issues that came up from her story of victimization. Each time a thought hooked her and emotions flooded her awareness, she paused and leaned into them, using therapeutic mindfulness. She described the feelings in her body and allowed them room to express themselves. Sandy repeated the process until there were no more strong emotions on the surface to work through. She was then able to face her ex and deal with the logistics of divorce in a calm and rational manner.

If you are able not to be pulled into jerk brain's story, then you can watch the thoughts with a sense of detachment. When a strong emotional reaction comes up, simply pause the narrative and focus completely on the emotion in your body using the body focusing questions from the basic protocol. With this skill set, you can work through complicated issues one trigger at a time.

During therapeutic mindfulness, you could occasionally have a memory or a deep insight, or a sense of knowing pop up. This is different from the victimization story that jerk brain thrives on. Insight and knowing feels calm and steady.

No matter what comes up, your response should be the same. You can acknowledge what popped up, then return to the process of describing and allowing. A memory popping up is fine, so long as it is observed with nonjudgment, and then you return to describing and allowing.

I was doing a session of therapeutic mindfulness with myself. Typically, I have a choked feeling in my throat or a cloudy tightness in my chest. This time, the feeling manifested as a vivid sensation like a saw blade piercing through the top of my skull on the left side. As I followed the moving sensation with open curiosity, it culminated in a painful spike as if someone were stabbing my left eye. I stayed open to the experience. A memory from my youth flashed when a smaller child threatened to stab me in the eye with a pencil. I remember having some fear because I believed my strength couldn't protect me if I was caught off guard.

This session showed me that I had carried that image of violence with me into adulthood. I did not analyze what this meant during my mindfulness practice. Instead, I acknowledged the memory and then focused on my body, allowing the physical sensation to continue until it resolved.

As a side note, when resolving issues like this, there is no danger of letting your guard down and becoming naive. Healing does not remove survival instinct, only pain.

This is an example of an image, memory, or insight bubbling to the surface. I did not encourage a monologue in my head to explore why the memory arose. I noticed the memory and then focused on how my body was expressing it. I continued to be with the sensations, describing them as they changed within my body.

When something pops up during the process, it can be acknowledged, but it is important not to slip back into thought spirals. In this process, always return to the body. Only afterward did I allow myself to consider how this memory had impacted my adult life. When people have the urge to analyze during therapeutic mindfulness, I remind them that they may analyze to their heart's content for the next six days and twenty-three hours!

Exercise 10. Processing a Story with Therapeutic Mindfulness

1. Find a subject your mind likes to rant about that brings up strong emotions.

2. Begin thinking about your subject in your typical way but be on the lookout for any thought that brings with it a stab of painful emotion.

3. When the emotion spikes, stop! Do therapeutic mindfulness. Notice:

   ◦ What do you feel?

   ◦ Where is it in your body?

   ◦ Ask yourself the body focusing questions to get super clear and focused on the body sensations. (Do step 2: Describe.)

   ◦ Remind yourself to lean in using your favorite allowing phrases from the worksheet. (Do step 3: Allow.)

   ◦ Continue to describe and allow until the emotion subsides.

4. Check in with the thought that brought up the strong emotion. If more emo-

tion comes up, you can keep working with it. If the emotion is gone or minimal, move to step 5.

5. Begin again by letting your story run through your mind, looking for more thoughts that cause a spike of emotion.

6. Repeat this process as long as you have strong emotions or until your time or energy runs out for this mindfulness session.

Using the Second Person on the Allowing Phrases

For many people, it is revolutionary to see their negative emotions as a hurt part of them and to allow it to be there. Notice that the allowing phrases do this by speaking to the hurt part in the third person. I suggest such phrases as the following:

- "Let it be there."

- "Give it space."

- "Notice it is a hurt part of you."

If you feel comfortable expressing compassion for your hurt parts, you can use the allowing phrases in the second person. After you've described the feelings using the body focusing questions, use the same ideas from the allowing phrases but speak directly to the feeling. You can say the following:

- "You're allowed to be here."

- "Take all the space you need."

- "I see you are hurt. I'm here with you."

If this doesn't feel right for you, don't worry! It is very effective to stick to the allowing phrases as they are. Don't force this if it feels insincere. However, if this feels okay, try it. There is something intimate and nurturing about speaking directly to your hurts in a fully accepting way.

For more ideas, use the worksheet "Alternative Allowing Phrases in Second Person" (see the Appendix).

Enhancing Results with Radical Allowing

While I mentioned this before, it is worth bringing up again, specifically in the context of advanced therapeutic mindfulness techniques.

If you have found that you can tolerate the process without help, then here's a pro tip: invite the feeling to get worse! This probably sounds weird, but seriously, try it. If the feeling is heavy, ask it how heavy it needs to get. If it is hot, ask if it needs to get hotter. If it is cold, invite it to show you how cold it truly feels. Use this process if the feeling is tight, dark, or pressured. Even if it feels like stabbing, ask it how painful it needs to get. Then allow all of it to be there.

Essentially, you are letting the feeling know it will be heard no matter how unacceptable it thinks it is.

Inviting the feeling to get worse is the closest thing I have found to a shortcut. It gives you a great ability to know the power of allowing and to learn that you can be okay even when feeling bad. If this feels right for you, try it! This habit will greatly enhance how quickly you process emotions as well as your confidence in your ability to do hard things.

Enhancing Positive Emotions with Therapeutic Mindfulness

When you do therapeutic mindfulness and a feeling becomes less intense, keep going! Continue as long as your higher self says you have the energy to do so—or as long as your worldly self says you have the time! There is more depth in the healing if you see it through to completion. Sometimes other layers of emotion come up, or sometimes you get to feel calm and peaceful.

When all the negative feeling has disappeared, you can enhance your results by simply continuing. Most people seem to have an impulse to stop once they no longer feel bad. However, I think you should stick around. There is power in staying emotionally connected to the deep peace that comes after healing.

When you have this opportunity, return to the Describe -> Allow cycle but focus now on the pleasant feelings. You might find openness in your breathing and relaxed muscles. You might have a light feeling in your chest or head. You might have a sense of relief.

Whatever you identify, notice that, and continue to allow yourself to be with your body experience. This part should feel really, really good. As always, stay connected to your body and don't try to think. Just experience.

This is also a time when you could have spontaneous positive thoughts, but instead of trying to talk yourself into believing them, now you simply feel their truth. Healing images could also pop up. Keep noticing all these things without judgment: let them sink in and enjoy them. Simply getting an experience of peace and contentment gives you a break from the stress you were carrying before. It also reinforces your brain's ability to be peaceful. If you want peace, don't underestimate this part of the practice! Take the time to sit with the feeling of peace mindfully and allow it to sink deep into your mind.

CHAPTER FOURTEEN

POSITIVE PSYCHOLOGY

You might wonder, "If therapeutic mindfulness is so powerful, is this the only tool I need?" Or, "Are the other tools I've learned a waste of time?"

Absolutely not! Surprisingly, I did not invent healing! Throughout time, healers have taught different methods of healing and growth. There are valuable approaches to mind training and there are useful positive skills. You might have learned tools from a parent, teacher, friend, therapist, boss, book, speaker, or online source. Yet the mind is so tricky and so persistent in its attempts to avoid feeling, it will misuse tools to deny and ignore feelings. It wants the shortcut and the dramatic transformation. It certainly doesn't want to be uncomfortable and vulnerable!

This book is designed specifically to address a gaping hole in the modern Western healing mindset. It focuses on how to work with the hard stuff. It teaches about reducing avoidance and cultivating nonjudgment. It strives to remove fears that block the positive tools from working. For those unfamiliar, this chapter will touch on some positive psychology tools. This is not an exhaustive list, but a very basic introduction. Of course, these tools are most helpful when you can spot avoidance and work through hard feelings.

Different people experience positive effects from different activities or sources. They might respond well when they build things, fix cars, do crafts, spend time in nature, color, sing, garden, cook, clean, listen to sermons, listen to inspirational speakers, read, meditate, pray, take long showers, or spend time with friends.

Because people respond differently, it is good to explore what activities and tools fit your temperament and personality. What follows is a limited discussion of positive psychology tools.

Work with the Dark and the Light

On the surface, it seems to make sense to tell yourself only positive things. It's all about your attitude, right?

I disagree. From what I've seen, it's all about the Core Belief. When your *Core Belief* is that you can't face the dark stuff, hiding from it with positive words reinforces your fear of the dark. It is more effective to acknowledge the negative and then reinforce the positive. One client learned this the hard way:

> Diana described how she had created a happy mindset lasting more than a year. She invested time in reciting positive affirmations and practicing calming meditations, and she focused on the positive things in her life. It seemed to be working. Her mood was generally good, and she was functioning well.
>
> Then Diana's boyfriend broke up with her. She was devastated. Her devastation went far beyond what she might have expected from a breakup of a short-term relationship. As we explored the breakup, Diana started making connections to unresolved grief for her father. She noticed how her boyfriend's mannerisms resembled her father's. Both the relationship and the breakup reminded her of the rejection she'd felt from her father at times. In fact, Diana's reactions to the breakup didn't seem to be about her boyfriend at all!
>
> As we continued therapy, it became clear that the loss of her boyfriend had triggered grief over her father's death and the hurts she still carried about their relationship. Once this grief was triggered, it overwhelmed her. Diana sank into a persistent depression. Years of unexamined thoughts, beliefs, and emotions were all coming out at once. On top of this, her

belief in God (whom she'd used in her affirmations for the past year) suffered, and her belief in her ability to heal was damaged.

As we worked together, Diana could see that her attempt to create her happiness was well-meaning but incomplete. She understood how her avoidance had stored up all of her pain. The pain was waiting for a chance to come out. With this knowledge, she was able to begin facing her emotions and working toward happiness in a more realistic way.

Diana's depression was a result of working very diligently with the positive tools but ignoring her negative feelings. She demonstrated several great traits: self-sufficiency, determination, and persistence. She worked her tush off! The positive tools felt good because they are useful—but not by themselves. She needed to spend time with the hard stuff—her feelings about her father.

I sometimes help clients put the negative stuff on the shelf, but not for months or years. It's fine to shelve it long enough to get out of the grocery store, put the kids to bed, and get some time to yourself—or until your next therapy appointment in a few days.

So long as you are working on your dark side, your mind is relieved. It knows you're doing the work. It knows the difference between taking a break and running for the hills. Then when you tell your mind positive things, it is more willing to believe them because it knows you can handle the hard things. Working on the tough stuff develops core beliefs such as the following:

- I am stronger than these feelings.

- I can do hard things.

- Healing is possible.

- I am capable.

- Pain does not define me.

- I am more than my pain.

- I can persevere and grow.

These beliefs are anti-fear. This is why practicing therapeutic mindfulness helps conquer debilitating emotions.

As this chapter reviews tools and skills, notice that for each tool, it is important to use what you've learned in this book (and practiced by now, right?) to pause when you catch your mind avoiding something. When working on the positive, negative responses can come up. The healthy choice is either to work on the negative right away or to write it down and work on it during your next session of therapeutic mindfulness. Such moments are great opportunities to delve into your feelings with open curiosity and nonjudgment. Getting to the other side of the negative reaction will clear the way for that positive tool to start working.

In this way, therapeutic mindfulness can make all other tools more powerful by removing emotional blocks and allowing the tools to work. This is how you work with both the dark and the light parts of your mind.

Challenging Your Thoughts

Perhaps you have heard of cognitive behavioral therapy or CBT. A central function of CBT is to challenge thinking.

Remember that trying to fix yourself with thoughts can lead to feeling worse and worse—as described in the "Wallow" section of chapter 3. Our default way of thinking gets us in more trouble unless we have learned how to shift perspectives on our own. For this reason, other people's thoughts are useful—in particular, the thoughts of wise people who help you ease your judgments.

To find such influences, look for people who know peace and happiness. These could be people you know or books you read. Either way, if you feel more peaceful after hearing their words, that's a sign that this is a good resource for you.

As a young adult, my growth took off when I learned different ways of thinking about life. Certain people and books influenced me to not be a victim in my own story. Believing I could influence my life and become happier led me to act. I began cultivating ways of thinking that felt better and exploring the wisdom of others.

Sometimes we're stuck in ways of thinking that keep us unhappy. In just one example of many, black-and-white thinking is a common negative mental habit that therapists will tackle for those who haven't yet learned to question their thinking. Here's an example from a client of mine:

> At the beginning of her therapy, Emily would share frustrations about her life. As she spoke, I noticed a constant barrage of unfounded assumptions about herself, others, and the future. It seems that all I did for six months was ask, "Is that true?"
>
> Emily and I had a good enough therapeutic relationship that she knew I wasn't asking in judgment. She was open and would explore the question. Often, I had to direct her to the emotions that lie underneath her thinking as well as point out other possible interpretations of her narrative.
>
> After working together for a while, Emily developed the habit of checking her own jerk brain story rather than believing any thought she had. Often she would tell me something, then pause and say, "No, that's not true." For example, if she said something like, "If I try that, I know I'll fail," then she would pause and say, "No, that's not true. I realize I said that because I'm scared to put myself out there."

In this example, you can see how core beliefs create your attitudes about the world. If all your thinking reinforces core beliefs like, "I'm not good enough," and, "People are cruel," you will be stuck in an unhappy life. Many self-help books are geared toward exploring different ways of thinking to help you shift your viewpoint. This won't heal deep trauma, but it is a great way to catch your jerk brain feeding you junk and replace that junk with thoughts that help.

Therapeutic mindfulness is great for emotional reactions that feel stuck, but it does not directly address habits of thinking. You can learn to catch automatic negative thinking habits and replace them with better habits.

One useful version of this is called *REBT therapy* by Dr. Albert Ellis. If you look up "REBT irrational beliefs," you will find common beliefs that pop up automatically for many of us. Learning common dysfunctional ways of thinking can help you realize that you're not alone nor are you bad for thinking these things. This is just one way our brain works.

Knowing and catching the patterns helps you believe them less. Just because you have the thought doesn't mean you have to believe the thought!

Here's an example of the good that can come from shifting perspective:

Sophia had such crippling social anxiety that her voice would tremble when she ordered coffee at a drive-through window. A spiral of negative thoughts would accost her at the slightest glance of a stranger. She was afraid of being judged for her perceived weaknesses and defects.

I helped her start practicing a strategy for changing her story. We started with a basic trigger, such as a woman glancing at her. We brainstormed many possibilities for what could be happening. Here are the types of ideas we came up with:

- The woman was judging her but only to avoid her own painful self-judgment.
- The woman was checking out her awesome fashion sense!
- The woman was hoping Sophia did not see her defects and was desperate to look calm and normal. (This is common!)
- The woman was being remotely controlled by aliens and scanning all nearby life forms. (Hey, it's okay to have fun with this!)
- The woman wondered if she recognized Sophia but quickly looked away so she wouldn't be caught staring.

I had her try this on situations that came up in her life. After practicing for a while, Sophia shared some victories where she no longer took an interaction as a personal attack—even when the stranger was rude or looked mean.

Less than a year later, Sophia and I were working on other things when she attended a wedding. Later that evening she cried happy tears because she had a great time—which was a foreign experience. She realized only after the wedding that she had forgotten to be anxious!

Any method you can use to *depersonalize* your thinking is helpful. Taking things personally is one of the biggest mental habits that cause us pain. This is unfortunate since nothing is ever personal.

Any method you can use to judge yourself less and to be gentle instead is helpful. The entirety of chapter 9 in this book is focused on challenging your old way of thinking about yourself and shifting your mindset to one of self-compassion.

Another great resource for catching and questioning unhelpful thoughts is *The Work* by Byron Katie. She has several books and many YouTube videos that depict her working actively with people at seminars on their negative thoughts. She brings humor, wisdom, and deep compassion while absolutely debunking her attendees' jerk brain stories. Other helpful authors are Richard Carlson, Deepak Chopra, Melanie Beattie, Pema Chodron, and Lindsay Gibson.

There are many wise people who can guide us on our path; it's a matter of finding who speaks to you. Of course, when you are working with logic but run into negative emotional reactions that don't budge, you can shift to therapeutic mindfulness to clear the parts of you that are stuck.

When you do find ideas that help you feel better, you can absorb them more deeply into your mind when you pause, reflect, and notice the impact on your mind and body.

I would suggest that as you read self-help books or watch inspirational speakers (or talk to a wise friend/therapist), you write down thoughts that are especially helpful. Then try this exercise:

Exercise 11. Deepening Positive Thoughts

1. Choose a helpful idea that you wish to understand or believe more deeply.

2. Repeat the idea slowly a few times, out loud if helpful.

3. Notice how your mind feels when you repeat the thought. Is it resisting and combative? Or does it become calm? (If there is resistance, then this is a good target for therapeutic mindfulness.)

4. If it is calm, notice how your body feels in more detail as you repeat the thought. What do you notice in your head, jaw, neck, shoulders, chest, arms, stomach, and legs? Scan down your body for feelings, including whether muscles are more or less relaxed.

5. Without trying to change it, notice how your breathing feels when repeating this thought.

6. Because the thought is peaceful, allow your mind to explore where this thought is true for you personally, staying in touch with body reactions and emotions that come up. You could find yourself feeling calm, peaceful, and happy.

7. Continue to reinforce the thought or just sit with the calmness in your body as long as desired, repeating the thought occasionally and enjoying your peaceful time.

Other Therapy Tools

This section shares some general ideas that are useful for mental health. The list can get you started if you're new to working on yourself.

Fill the Tank

When I get a new client who says she is always overwhelmed, the first thing I check is whether she can say no or if she is caught up in people-pleasing. People pleasers might squeeze out one hour a week (if that) for therapy, but it can be difficult to make progress when she doesn't implement changes. Making a change for herself means saying no to something she "should" be doing for someone else – which for her means guilt, fear, abandonment, or feeling like a bad, selfish person.

It might be hard to hear this, but spending time on yourself is an indispensable part of mental health. People want to skip this requirement, but it is mandatory. Perhaps an illustration will help.

Imagine that you have an amazing weekend. Maybe it's a weekend filled with quality time with close friends or time working on a hobby or having a favorite getaway. It can include a spa day, time on the golf course, or whatever fills your tank. At the end of the weekend, you feel relaxed and content. You return home and see that your dog has chewed up a favorite piece of furniture. Then you go into the living room and find your child has poured pancake flour and syrup all over the living room carpet and rubbed it in.

Think about what you might feel, think, and do. After being in that contented, peaceful space, is it easier to respond calmly? Think about whether you'd be able to rein in your negative reaction. Pause and reflect.

Now, start again. Imagine you just finished a disastrous week of work. Absolutely everything went wrong. You felt exhausted and frustrated and doubted your job security. A coworker was actively undermining you while you tried to keep things together, and you felt close to snapping. (Feel free to fill in your own details.) In addition, you've been having an ongoing argument with a difficult family member. Finally, it's Friday night. You come home and see your dog has chewed up a favorite piece of furniture. Then you go into the living room and find your child has poured pancake flour and syrup all over the living room carpet and rubbed it in.

Think about what you might feel, think, and do. Can you sense a difference in how you would respond, both in your mind and your behavior? Pause and reflect.

Filling our tank is not about being selfish—it's about having the fuel to be better humans with those we love, work with, and see out in the world. The *No Guilt Mom* podcast has a saying: "A good mom is a happy mom." When our tank is full, we can be our best selves. But we must take time to do the things that make life enjoyable.

If you're not used to taking care of yourself, remember that time spent doing something fun or relaxing can be extremely uncomfortable as the guilt assails you with questions about what you should be doing and who you're letting down. These feelings are powerful subjects for therapeutic mindfulness. Working through guilt and fear leads to a more peaceful you. When you learn to be peaceful, that is a lesson you teach by example to the people around you.

If you believe you should take care of yourself but cannot seem to make yourself do so, there is some deep work to be done. Therapeutic mindfulness can be helpful, but I recommend pursuing EMDR therapy on memories from childhood related to low self-esteem or the need to perform and please others.

If you are able to step back from this compulsion and take care of yourself, this means you believe that you truly matter. Check in with your intuition. You know when you need self-care. You know what it feels like when your tank is empty or full. You know what it feels like when you're getting perilously low on emotional energy. That's when it's time to do the things in life that fill your tank. This could mean taking alone time, or it could mean socializing or doing a favorite hobby or things that remind you of a purpose you hold dear.

Quick note: Watching TV and using social media do not count as self-care. Many people who are overwhelmed try to escape into these mediums. However, whatever emotions you want to escape from typically come back within seconds of stopping these activities. I have nothing against binging a good show or watching silly videos—if there's fuel in the tank. Yes, these things are engrossing enough to temporarily squash the guilt, which is why people pleasers can spend time this way. This does not, however, fill the tank, and it will not help with that sense of being overwhelmed.

If you're not sure what things fill up your tank, you can explore ideas by searching online. *Dialectical behavioral therapy* (DBT) has great worksheets to help. Try searching the term: "DBT list of pleasurable activities." This is a quick way to explore activities that might feed you. For example, do you feel recharged when cooking, when creating art or music, when connecting to others, or when focusing on your spiritual life?

Some people have ideas about the things they're "supposed" to do to take care of themselves, but it is important to find what truly fills your tank. Some people feel like they are "supposed to" exercise to take care of themselves. Check in with yourself. I have two friends who get very stressed if they don't exercise. The gym is their happy place. Most people I know are not like that! For many people, going to the gym takes willpower and energy. Similarly, some people feel good when they socialize, while others need more time alone.

Whatever ideas you try, check in with yourself. After the activity, is your tank fuller, or did you use up energy? Do you have more or less to give afterward? Your answers are inside you.

When exploring activities, it can be very helpful to check whether there are major areas in your life where you feel a deficit. Consider this list of life categories:

- Religious/spiritual

- Life purpose

- Work/money

- Intellectual

- Health/Fitness

- Home environment

- Hobbies/fun

- Social time

- Family

- Romantic relationships

- Creativity

Not every category is important to every person. If you're struggling to understand where you need to make a change to fill your needs, I recommend the following exercise.

Exercise 12. Life Balance

Use the list of life categories above:

1. Check each item that is important for you to have in your life.

2. Star each item that is absolutely vital to have in your life based on your values (not on what others think you should do).

3. Choose a starred item. Ask yourself, "Am I getting enough of this in my life?" The right answer will come from a place of knowing, not from a place of "I should do more." Check with your inner wisdom—it has the answer.

4. Repeat this with all starred items. Your gut will give you very quick and clear feedback when you are missing something you need for self-care.

5. For any starred items that have a major deficit, brainstorm what would correct this.

6. Choose the most important change to make today. Make only one or two changes at a time until those changes feel like a solid part of your life routine.

7. Return to make other changes as desired. First, make changes to your starred items. Then move on to checked items until your tank feels full.

*Note: If you find that you're putting a lot of effort into an item that is not checked or starred, this is good information about where you ought to lower your expenditure of time and energy.

For additional resources on this topic, the book *Boundaries* by Henry Cloud and John Townsend is remarkable at explaining the issues around saying no. It is a Christian-based psychology book, but you don't have to be Christian to gain insight from it. The psychology principles are insightful and practical, and I recommend it to anyone needing help with boundaries. It is especially good for people who believe being Christian means you should never say no. For a secular book, check out *Codependent No More* or *The New Codependency*, both by Melanie Beattie.

Spending time on the things that bring joy in life might sound like obvious advice for a happy life, but so often it is the first thing to be dropped from the list of priorities for people who are unhappy. They can't bring themselves to say no, cancel appointments, or leave work on time. Other things seem more important because they appear to be more urgent. While self-care is generally not urgent, make no mistake: it is necessary. People who are happier have learned this. They see the wisdom in scheduling time for themselves and keeping that appointment!

In short, give yourself permission to take care of yourself. Then make it a mandate.

Emotional Regulation

If you struggle to control your basic emotions in day-to-day life, I do recommend brief therapy to learn some basic tools. It is sometimes helpful to have those tools personalized to your situation. A therapist versed in dialectical behavioral therapy (DBT) or trauma could have what you need. While it's most helpful to work directly with a professional in the beginning, books and homework can move you along in between sessions. Ask your therapist for recommendations.

After trying any tool, whether recommended by a book or a therapist, use your place of knowing, your intuition, to see if it is a good tool for you. If not, you might need more instruction, or you might realize that something else altogether is a better fit for your needs and personality.

Basic Affirmations

Repeating daily affirmations is a common tool suggested in both therapy and the self-help world. However, affirmations can be used to negative effect, as in the case of Diana at the beginning of this chapter. Let's look more closely at affirmations and how to make them useful.

Once when I led a therapy group, a participant said her individual therapist gave her a list of affirmations. When asked to share one of her favorites, she perused the list and then read, "Everything is getting better every day."

I think the muscle above my left eyeball started twitching.

In all seriousness, I pulled my best poker face as I listened, and then I decided to teach about affirmations. Why? Affirmations don't work if we believe they are an absolute lie. Did you believe that affirmation? Is everything getting better every day? What happens on the day a loved one dies? Or the day your country goes to war? How about the day you're fired and have no money? Will your brain believe it got better?

Life has ups and downs. Affirmation should help us when things go wrong. Unrealistic affirmations set the believer up to fail.

The first rule of affirmations is that at least part of your brain must believe it is possible. The above affirmation relies entirely upon external circumstances—which are always changing. This is as precarious as a house of cards. At the first gust of wind, the house of cards will crumble.

If we need the world to be perfect for us to be okay, then happiness will be a lost cause. Look around. The world is far from perfect. The only chance we have for happiness is to learn how to be okay despite the clear fact that we are not in paradise. Happily, this is possible. And people who feel good inside have more fuel to help our troubled world. Affirmations are the most potent when they focus on internal factors, such as growth and resilience.

Another common issue is all-or-nothing statements, which lead to the affirmations being unbelievable to the mind. For example:

"I am a good person."

"People are kind."

"Things always turn out for the best."

"Life is wonderful."

When you read these, can you feel a skeptical part of yourself raising an eyebrow? If so, good! This means you can vet affirmations to see if they are true for you personally. If you want to believe some of the things on this list, it is more realistic to acknowledge that while not everything is perfect, you can still notice and appreciate the positive. Similar statements without the black-and-white thinking are as follows:

- "I am learning to appreciate the ways I am good."

- "I'm becoming gentler with myself when I make mistakes."

- "More and more, I can see good things in others, even when they have bad moments."

- "I am learning to appreciate pleasant things and roll with unpleasant things."

- "More and more I can see my resilience in the face of difficulty."

Notice that these examples focus on internal factors and include gray areas. They create room for growth. Another tip for creating useful affirmations is to use ones that acknowledge something that feels negative and then emphasize love and acceptance. Remember how important self-compassion is? You should consider whether an affirmation like this works for you. The basic formula is as follows:

- "Even though I _____, I'm learning to love and accept myself."

For example, you could say:

- "Even though I make mistakes, I'm learning to love and accept myself."

Everyone doesn't respond the same to a given affirmation, but you can check with your inner knowing to see which ones feel right for you.

When you try an affirmation, such as, "I am learning to appreciate the ways I am good," you can ask yourself what percentage of you believes it is true. By this, I mean you must believe it emotionally. Does it *feel* true *to* you? This is different from thinking it is true. You can acknowledge the part of you that doesn't believe it and the part that does.

Consider this affirmation: "I'm learning to see the good in myself, even though I make mistakes." Does 60 percent of you believe it? Is 40 percent of you skeptical? When you reflect on this affirmation, does it help you connect to the ways that you *do* see good in yourself? If so, then this is an effective affirmation for you.

Spending time with an affirmation will help it to grow within you. Slow down. You're nourishing an important part of yourself. Notice ways that your affirmation seems true. Let these thoughts and images sink in as you reflect. Your mind will guide you. This is how you use an affirmation to shift your beliefs.

One common pitfall is to rattle off affirmations the way you would recite the alphabet.

> Eliza felt drawn to affirmations, so I helped her personalize a few of them. She practiced them diligently for a few weeks and shared that they were improving her mood and outlook.
>
> About two months later in therapy, Eliza was struggling with her deteriorating mood. She said she was still doing her affirmations daily, but they had stopped working. After a few questions, I learned that she had stopped pausing to reflect on them. They'd become mere words.
>
> I reminded her about slowing down with the affirmations and guided her to reflect on some of them in session with me. This helped. Spending time on the affirmations helped shift her to thinking more positively about herself. By using affirmations this way, they "worked" again.

When people recite an affirmation without pausing to reflect, the words become meaningless. They might as well recite multiplication tables. By slowing down and really noticing how the statements feel true for you, you help the words sink more deeply into your mind and your belief system. Using the affirmations in times when you need them also trains your brain in the habit of remembering helpful ideas in your daily life.

Because it's best to slow down and reflect, you don't need a lot of affirmations. I would suggest making a list of ten or fewer affirmations. You might work with only four. You might pick one at a time and do a fifteen-minute contemplation on that statement alone. You can experiment and find what works for you.

Summary of tips for using affirmations:

1. **Emphasize inner traits instead of external circumstances**. It is wonderful to practice gratitude toward the gifts of life. However, making our happiness dependent on those circumstances means our happiness can be taken away in a moment. It is far more powerful to emphasize your ability to appreciate positive things and to bounce back when you experience negative things.

2. **Go for shades of gray instead of black and white**. One way to do this easily is to use the phrases "I'm learning" or "More and more" at the beginning to show movement or progress. "I'm learning to see good in myself," is much more believable than, "I am good." We all have good and bad moments. We can acknowledge this while noticing the good.

3. **Practice affirmations with mindfulness**. After saying each affirmation, pause a moment and reflect. You might even repeat it several times. How does it feel in your body when you say it? What related ideas come to mind? Where is it true for you? You can even close your eyes and use meditation music. You might wish to pause briefly on one affirmation but linger for quite a while on another as you intuitively notice what your mind needs.

If you try affirmations and some negative things come up, that is information about where some healing work can be done using therapeutic mindfulness.

I was first introduced to affirmations by listening to a recording of Belleruth Knaperstak, who is one of the early industry leaders in trauma research. The recording had meditative music over which she would slowly say an affirmation, pause for several moments, and then move on to the next one. She went through the whole list twice for a total of about twenty minutes. By the time I was finished listening, I would feel very relaxed and clearheaded. You can replicate this with your personal affirmations, creating a very calming and healing routine.

Affirmations are meant to be repeated over time to help the ideas become part of your habit of thinking. Your jerk brain spews negative thoughts automatically every day. The opposite of jerk brain thinking is to train your brain by practicing positive thoughts daily. Affirmations are about you taking back your power of thought.

Focused Affirmations for Growth

Affirmations can be focused on improving your view of yourself. They can also be used to train your mind to think in ways you would prefer, whether you want to be more patient or focused, have stronger faith, etcetera. Christians use daily devotionals to increase faith. Buddhists actively work on building traits like compassion using contemplation practices.

Anytime you gain helpful ideas from reading a self-help book, watching an inspiring speaker, or having a conversation that moves you, you can use the ideas to create affirmations. You can also deepen the ideas by journaling, or through meditation.

All useful ideas must be repeated for us to shift our mindset. This is one reason it is helpful to spend time with wise people, even if we've heard their ideas before. Remember how often your negative ideas are in your head. It takes far less repetition for positive thoughts to have a powerful influence on the mind. Ideas are more powerful when you *pause and notice*. When jerk brain tells you something terrible, you have an emotional reaction to it. You can also notice a positive emotional reaction to affirmations.

For example, if you want to become kinder to yourself and others, you might read through chapter 9 on compassion and write down helpful concepts. Use those ideas as you would affirmations, or choose one to sit quietly with and explore in contemplative meditation. While contemplative meditation is beyond the scope of this book, it is a worthy subject to research if you want to deepen your practice beyond affirmations.

I recommend finding time daily to do your preferred practice. Even five minutes daily makes a mark. For extra mind training, you can put a sticky note on your desk or have a reminder pop up on your calendar each hour to remind you of a useful idea that you want to turn into a thinking habit. Reflecting on it during the day helps you train your brain and apply the idea in your life.

Regular reflection on thoughts that instill compassion or wisdom can lead to other life perspective changes. For example, if you are practicing thoughts about not taking things personally, this could apply to every interaction. When a coworker gets snippy, you might see his frustration with compassion and know his mood is not about you. When you come across an aggressive driver, you might consider how stressful it is to live a life where you are always hurried, rushing, and not at peace.

One book with effective ideas about shifting perspective is *Don't Sweat the Small Stuff* by Richard Carlson. Books like these have a fountain of useful ideas. A book that explores a different way of seeing life from our Western perspective is *The Art of Happiness* by the

Dalai Lama. Of course, you can always ask people you respect for books they've found transformative or valuable.

Remember not to get caught up in perfection. If you mean to practice a thought hourly and end up reviewing it only a few times a day, that is still a few times more than you did before. This is far better than letting your jerk brain take up all your mental space!

Whatever religion or philosophy you follow, even if you just want to be a consistently kind person, you must apply those valuable ideas in your daily life situations. Affirmations are a way to remember those ideas when you need to apply them. Here's one person who used affirmations effectively:

> Sara was in a year-long drug and mental health recovery program. This was not her first time, and the staff didn't think her chances were high. I met with Sara weekly. For the first month, Sara cried on and off throughout the session. Her depression was palpable. She was drawn to using affirmations, so we customized some, and she wrote them on index cards. When she had a break during the daytime, she would go through her cards, one by one, reading the affirmations.

> For problems this complex, there are many ways a program tries to help foster sobriety, yet affirmations were a key tool for Sara. At the end of the three months, her transformation was dramatic. Sara smiled throughout the session. Her whole demeanor had changed. Much later in the program, her closest friend relapsed, but she stayed strong in sobriety.

> Sara seemed to hold onto the affirmations like a rock to keep herself on track as she went through the program. She worked hard, and her determination showed. Affirmations had helped her train her mind to think more positively. I was very pleased to attend her graduation when she finished the program drug-free.

As discussed earlier, building compassion for yourself is central to your ability to heal. You can use affirmations to assist in developing self-compassion. While this idea of being gentle with ourselves is simple, we are often so trained in negative thinking that we need to practice kind thoughts. These thoughts should be repeated so often that we create a habit of thinking this way. To combat the negative thoughts on autopilot, we need to bring helpful thoughts into our all-day thinking pattern.

If you have a specific goal, you could choose one affirmation and use it as a mantra—a statement used again and again to train your mind.

Exercise 13a. Self-Acceptance Mantra

1. Write down the judgments you use most often against yourself.

2. Write down a simple phrase that could be used as a mantra (a phrase repeated often to remind yourself of a new way of thinking. See Exercise 13b – Supplement, for tips on creating your mantra.)

3. Take five minutes first thing in the morning and last thing at night to repeat your mantra slowly and notice supporting thoughts or positive feelings that come up in response to this mantra.

   ◦ Note: If strong negative thoughts or feelings arise, save those as targets for therapeutic mindfulness. You should spend time working through the negative reaction before trying to use this mantra.

4. For the first few weeks, set up a reminder to pop up on your phone with the mantra every hour of the day. When you're able, pause for a breath as you recite the mantra and notice how it feels.

   ◦ Note: If you miss the reminder several times during the day, you still receive great benefits each time you can pause with your mantra, so long as you don't judge yourself for missing it. This is also a great opportunity to be gentle with yourself if you think you should do this "perfectly."

Exercise 13b. – Supplement: How to Create a Mantra

Look through the list of judgments you wrote. You might notice themes or find a statement that stands out as particularly painful. Consider such self-defeating ideas as the following:

- "I'm weak for feeling this way."

- "If I ask for help, I'm weak."

- "Something is fundamentally wrong with me."

- "I'm a failure."

- "I'm bad/unworthy."

- "I'm stupid."

- "I should be over this already."

You could create your mantra by writing the opposite of the judgments you found. Here is a list of possible alternative statements for the ones above:

- "It takes strength to face hard feelings."

- "It takes courage to be vulnerable and ask for help."

- "I am a work in progress, like everyone else."

- "Failure is information for my improvement."

- "Although I have faults, I also have worth."

- "I'm learning, and that's okay."

- "The pain I have simply shows me where to focus my healing efforts."

You could also explore other sources of helpful thoughts, such as a book or a wise friend. You might want to explore inspirational sayings or quotes on a quality you wish to develop. Thoughts that leave you feeling more kind-hearted toward yourself and the world are good. If you don't already have thoughts like this, here are some ideas to help get you started:

- "I can make mistakes and still have value."

- "Authenticity is better than perfection."

- "Progress is real. Perfection is an illusion."

- "When I'm okay with being imperfect, I teach my kids (friends, family, coworkers, others) that it is okay to be imperfect."

- "I am learning. That means I'm still figuring things out, and that's okay."

- "I am still learning—just like everyone else."

- "When I check in with my past self, I can see how I'm learning and improving."

- "In spite of any faults, I see my positive qualities."

- "Dealing with hard things proves I am stronger than I was."

Mind Training, Meditation, and the Like

Any form of mind training can be used to create a happier, more stable self. In recent decades, ideas around meditation and mindfulness have spread through the Western world like wildfire. Scientists have used brain scan technology to study monks who are experienced in meditation. Multiple styles of therapy are built around such studies.

Most therapy tools I've seen fashioned from these practices are used in guided visualization-type exercises or used for calming down in the moment (i.e., coping). Coping skills are necessary for the short-term management of negative emotions.

Note the key phrase: *short-term*. Coping skills get you through the moment. Healing skills get you through life.

Coping skills get you through the moment.
Healing skills get you through life.

Guided visualization uses focus, relaxation, and imagination to put the mind into an altered state—this could be used for relaxation, healing, or exploration. These tools typically start with a mindful exercise, such as focusing on the breath or scanning the body. Then the listener is guided through a series of images. You might be guided to walk on a beach or meet a spirit guide or use healing light for illness. Visualizations can focus on physical healing, emotional healing, relieving anxiety or depression, contemplating God, and an endless variety of other topics.

You can find guided visualizations (also often called "guided meditations") by searching YouTube for any topic that you want help with or any image that feels peaceful. On YouTube, type "guided meditation" or "guided visualization" with any term you want to explore. Here are some ideas for what to search for:

- Guided meditation beach

- Guided meditation mountain

- Guided meditation waterfall

- Guided meditation forest

- Guided meditation spirit guide

- Guided meditation Christian

- Guided meditation let go, let God

- Guided meditation peace of God

- Guided meditation Jesus

- Guided meditation source

- Guided meditation chakra healing

- Guided meditation mantras

- Guided meditation loving kindness

- Guided meditation self-compassion

- Guided meditation acceptance

- Guided meditation anxiety

- Guided meditation depression

- Guided meditation self-love

- Guided meditation wisdom

Each of these searches will provide many options. You can explore and learn your preferences, such as whether you want to hear only a voice or prefer music to help you focus.

When practicing meditation and visualization, there are a host of physical and mental benefits. If you choose, this could also deepen your religious or spiritual practice. You can learn by practicing from the many options on YouTube, following your favorite teacher, or engaging in live programs that teach meditation. There are many options to help you spend time inside a peaceful mind. And, yes, there's an app for that! (Actually, there are many apps for that.)

If you're interested in learning about traditional meditation, there are good resources available. Teaching meditation is well beyond the scope of this book. However, you might start with some authors who teach the basics. Many Buddhists share these teachings freely, although there are secular and Christian meditators. You could explore authors and speakers such as Tara Brach, Pema Chodron, or Thich Nhat Hahn.

After building some proficiency in meditation, there is the option to expand your learning. Some people study at an ashram or join a society engaged in deep study such as Kriya Yoga. Yoga is for more than body exercises and could be a good complement to therapeutic mindfulness.

This book aims to teach people powerful ways to heal without the need to dedicate a life to meditation. Most people do not choose such a path, and yet most people need to learn how to heal. While there are more options, don't feel at all guilty if these do not call to you. Our job is to work on the next step of our healing and to walk our personal path, nothing more. Your intuition will tell you what feels right at this moment. That is all you need do.

CHAPTER FIFTEEN

CONCLUSION

If you're like many people, you have read through the whole book in one shot, and you probably have a good intellectual understanding of the material. Yet I must emphasize again the importance of experience. If you haven't already, I suggest you now go through the early exercises. Then begin a regular practice of therapeutic mindfulness. Find a schedule and commit. This could be something you do once a week or more often.

After you've tried it a few times, check in with how things are going. Are you quickly and easily making progress? If so, that's amazing! Keep it up until you find you're not sure what to do next. Then re-read parts of the book that can take you further, such as the chapter on core beliefs, resistance, or measuring progress.

Think of any reactions you would like to change. You could play with this by asking the magic question: "If I could wave a magic wand over myself and change an emotional reaction, what would I change?" This can guide you toward targets to work on. Or you could simply ask, "What bothers me every time it comes up?"

If you've tried therapeutic mindfulness a few times and found that you get stuck or have limited progress, I would suggest slowly re-reading all chapters after the description of how to do therapeutic mindfulness. This would mean starting at about chapter 5. You might have intuitive ideas about which areas you need help with, and you could return to those chapters instead. Perhaps you resonated with the discussion in chapter 9 on your hurt parts or chapter 11 on resistance. Read again slowly and apply the ideas to your practice as you improve your skill.

The information in this book is very dense in a way. The convoluted stories and avoidance tactics of the jerk brain could make it confusing and complicated for some people. However, the basic process of therapeutic mindfulness has a simplicity that will make it accessible to many people. The tools in this book are designed to help you find your way through the mists of jerk brain distractions and back to the fundamental methods of therapeutic mindfulness.

As a therapist, I see themes pop up again and again. Judgment blocks healing. Nurturing and compassion facilitate healing. We can only improve to the extent that we internalize compassion.

That's worth stating again: We can only improve to the extent that we internalize compassion. In the end, this book is a solution to avoidance as well as a practice of self-compassion.

I've written throughout the book about the chronic avoidance of feeling due to guilt, shame, and fear. The judgments of guilt and shame are central to everything. They keep us from internalizing compassion. If we avoid our pain, we cannot replace it with compassion. We fear that deep down we truly aren't worth the air we breathe. Yet, when we learn, bit by bit, to look at ourselves without judgment, we find the opposite to be true. Slowly, we release fear. We release judgment. We start to nurture ourselves and see our worth. Then we start to behave more like our true selves.

Therapeutic mindfulness helps separate your true self from those judgments. Through practicing therapeutic mindfulness, you learn to observe the hurts and fears that lie beneath your jerk brain story. Perhaps you view them at first with a sense of neutrality which helps keep you from being pulled into believing the judgments. Then over time, it becomes possible to see these aspects of your mind as they are: hurt, confused, and in pain. You begin to see your own simple humanity. Now self-compassion becomes possible.

When you ran from or condemned the parts that you couldn't handle, you gave yourself the message that those parts of you are unacceptable. By sitting with those parts, observing them, being kind and accepting, and watching them melt away, you give yourself the message that the hurt parts of you are worth nurturing. You become both a hurt child and a loving caregiver.

As your hurt parts heal, you will start to experience clarity. You will be able to hear your higher self without the chaos of jerk brain thinking. This practice can change your life.

I'm so very excited that you have explored these ideas with me. After seeing therapeutic mindfulness change people's lives for the better—and how it helps them no longer need my services as a therapist—I want to spread the word and help people gain the ability to nurture themselves through all that life throws at them. In learning this, I envision people teaching and nurturing their children, creating a ripple effect of kindness across generations.

May you find success on your path to a happier, healthier you.

THE END

APPENDIX

Daily Body Check-In

This simple but powerful exercise is a great start to your practice of therapeutic mindfulness. You can use it anytime, anyplace. It can increase emotional stability, body awareness and help reduce avoidance. Choose a time during the day when you can check in as part of your routine (i.e., after brushing your teeth or before leaving the car to go into work).

1. Pause. Ask yourself what you feel (positive or negative).

2. Ask yourself where you feel that in your body.

3. Describe the feeling.

4. Sit with the feeling for a few moments, just noticing but not trying to change anything.

5. Continue with your day.

*Daily practice increases emotional stability and awareness for many people.

Therapeutic Mindfulness How-To: Full Process

Step 1. Choose – A Target

1. If a strong emotion comes up, pause. You can begin immediately or once you are alone.

2. As part of a regular practice, choose any life situation, image, memory, or thought that brings up an illogical reaction or strong emotion. You can list these targets for future practice periods.

Step 2. Describe – Your Body Reactions

1. What do you feel, and where is it in your body?

2. Imagine the feeling is an entity that you can picture or sense. Ask the body focusing questions to get focused completely on the feeling.

Step 3. Allow – Practice Nonjudgment

1. Using the "Allowing Phrases" worksheet, repeat to yourself the phrases that fit best for you. Continue to repeat your phrases while paying attention to the feeling.

Step 4. Repeat – Steps 2 and 3

1. Every minute or so, use the body focusing questions to describe new changes.

2. After you describe, repeat your preferred allowing phrases.

Step 5. Return – To the Target

1. When the feeling has faded or disappeared, bring up the original thought, image, or memory that was emotional. Look directly at it and check for any lingering emotion.

2. If there is emotion left, you can return to steps 2 and 3 until you are done.

3. If there is no negative emotion, you can take a few moments to notice what it feels like in your body when you are calm and without that hurt.

Note: If you still have intense negative emotions when you're ready to finish, you can get back to your logical brain quickly by counting the things that you see. For example: Count everything you can see that is brown. Count everything that is square. Count how many shades of green you can find. You can also use your preferred coping and focusing skills (meditation, deep breathing, smelling a favorite scent, listening to music, gardening, time outdoors, snuggling with a pet, etcetera).

Body Focusing Questions

These questions help you get out of your thoughts and focused on your body to facilitate healing. Imagine the feeling is an entity that you can picture or imagine. Use these questions to describe the body feeling in more detail:

1. Where do you feel the sensation the most?

2. Describe the feeling. (Is it squeezing, tight, heavy, empty, moving, etc.?)

3. If it had a size, how big would it be?

4. If it had a color, what color would it be?

5. If it had a shape, what shape would it be?

6. If it had a temperature, what would that feel like?

7. If it had a texture, what would it feel like to touch?

8. If it had a weight, how heavy would it be?

9. Does it have a sense of movement, or is it lodged in place?

10. Is there a sense of aching or sharpness?

These questions root you in the body. If any of the questions do not have an answer (i.e., no sense of temperature), that's normal. Go to the next question.

Continue to describe the sensations as they change. Ask yourself the following:

Is the feeling becoming more or less? Is it better or worse or changing?

As the feeling shifts, keep describing it. Revisit the questions above. You may have odd impressions or feel it in places you don't expect, such as in your head or hands. Just continue to notice and sit with the discomfort.

Feeling "Stuck"

Ask all the questions again and see if any part of the feeling is shifting. If the feeling does not change in any way, allow it to be there a few minutes. If you still feel stuck, review chapter 8 for help troubleshooting or chapter 11 for help with resistance.

Allowing Phrases

Allowing phrases are designed to help you face discomfort in your body without judgment. Choose the phrases that feel best to you and say them to yourself when working through a difficult emotion.

- "Allow it to be there."

- "Let it be there, just for now."

- "Just notice."

- "Allow it space."

- "Open up to it."

- "I can let myself be uncomfortable."

- "I can let myself feel all of it."

- "Notice all of it."

- "My only job is to observe."

- "Try to let myself feel it, just for a few minutes."

- "Just be with it."

- "Watch it with open curiosity."

- "I care about this feeling."

- "Notice the part of me that feels it and the part that doesn't want to feel it."

- "Notice the part of me that needs to express this and the part of me that judges myself for feeling this. Just notice."

- "Remember, this is a hurt part of me that needs to be heard."

- "Notice that I am handling this. It's not too much. I am not too much."

- "My job is to hang out with the feeling. That's it. No need to analyze—I can do that later. Just be with it."

- "Do not try to *make* it better. The feeling just needs to be heard."

Alternative Allowing Phrases
in Second Person

This list shows what it looks like to speak directly to your hurt parts with compassion. The purpose is never to justify the hurt or to talk yourself into being allowed to feel, but rather to be nurturing to your own hurts the way you might for a loved one. Some people will feel better using the original "Allowing Phrases" worksheet, and that's okay. Always go with your intuition.

- "You're allowed to be here."

- "Take all the space you need."

- "I see you are hurt. I'm here with you."

- "I know it's hard to be going through this, but you don't have to do it alone."

- "You're not too much for me. I can be with you."

- "Do you need to get bigger?" "Do you need to get heavier?" (or other sensations: darker, hotter, colder, etcetera)

- "You can show up all the way. I'll stay with you."

- "I know you just need to be heard. I'm here."

- "I see you are uncomfortable. We can be uncomfortable together."

- "I will stay with you for a while."

- "I see how hard it is to be the part that has to hold everything together. I'm with you."

- "I won't try to change anything. I'm just here to listen to everything you want to share."

- "I know you don't get to express yourself often. That's why I'm here now."

- "I'm open to whatever you need to show me."

Allowing Phrases for Therapists

Allowing phrases are designed to help clients face discomfort in their bodies without judgment. Choose phrases that feel best in the situation. You can say them to clients while they are focusing on the feeling in their bodies.

- "Allow it to be there."

- "Let it be there, just for now."

- "Just notice."

- "Allow it space."

- "Open up to it."

- "Let yourself be uncomfortable."

- "Let yourself feel all of it."

- "Your only job is to observe."

- "See if you can let yourself feel it, just for a few minutes."

- "Just be with it."

- "Watch it with open curiosity." Or: "Be curious about what it will show you next."

- "You can say to yourself, 'I care about this feeling.'"

- "Notice the part of you that does feel it and the part that doesn't want to feel it."

- "Notice the part of you that needs to express this and the part of you that judges yourself for feeling this. Just notice."

- "Remember, this is a hurt part of you that needs to be heard."

- "Notice that you are handling it. It's not too much. You are not too much."

- "Your job is to hang out with the feeling. That's it. No need to analyze. [You, as the therapist, can do that later]. Just be with it."

- "Do not try to *make* it better. We never force a feeling. Instead, just listen. This is a very kind thing to do for your hurt part."

Progress Tracker

Date:

1. Trigger: What caused the strong reaction in you?

2. Thoughts: What were your thoughts about the situation?

3. Emotions: What were your emotions about the situation?

4. Body Reactions: What did you feel in your body in response to the situation?

5. Behaviors: What were your behaviors in reaction to the situation?

6. Core Beliefs: What did you believe about yourself in that triggered moment?

7. Duration: How long did your reaction last before you started feeling like your normal self?

8. Intensity: How intense did your reaction get? (You can use a scale from 1–10, 10 being the most intense reaction, or you can describe the intensity in your own words.)

9. Frequency: How long had it been since the last time you reacted this strongly?

ABOUT THE AUTHOR

Ruth Fearnow's first book, Therapeutic Mindfulness, is a synthesis of her decades-long meditation practice and her work as a trauma-focused therapist. As a Licensed Mental Health Counselor and Certified EMDR (Eye Movement Desensitization and Reprocessing) practitioner, she has identified and embedded the factors necessary for healing into therapeutic mindfulness, a skill to facilitate one's healing journey.

Ruth's private journey began as a young woman when she found herself studying kung fu and qi gong in Dengfeng City, China, the home of the famous Shaolin Temple. It was there she began a serious meditation practice. While this skill takes years to develop, this was her first big step to understanding mindfulness practices.

Ruth's evolution into a trauma therapist has enabled her to integrate age-old wisdom with trauma-informed insight. As a result, she has developed healing philosophies and the process of therapeutic mindfulness which she practices personally, and teaches to her clientele, many of whom use it on their own. Therapeutic mindfulness has now been adopted for professional use by colleagues in the mental health field.

Dealing with feelings directly is transformational and Therapeutic Mindfulness shows us *how* to do so. Ruth feels it is time to spread the word on a wide scale.

WEBSITE

If you've read this book and believe the message of Therapeutic Mindfulness should get out, please write a review the website where you purchased the book. To download the worksheets, get on my mailing list, inquire about speaking engagements or for updates on my work, go to www.ruthfearnow.com.

www.ingramcontent.com/pod-product-compliance
Lightning Source LLC
LaVergne TN
LVHW051517080426
835509LV00017B/2083